Home, I Am

Home, I Am

*A Minister's Metaphorical Memoir
on Midlife Meaninglessness*

Ferdinand Llenado

WIPF & STOCK · Eugene, Oregon

HOME, I AM
A Minister's Metaphorical Memoir on Midlife Meaninglessness

Copyright © 2012 Ferdinand Llenado. All rights reserved. Except for brief quotations in critical publications or reviews, no part of this book may be reproduced in any manner without prior written permission from the publisher. Write: Permissions, Wipf and Stock Publishers, 199 W. 8th Ave., Suite 3, Eugene, OR 97401.

Wipf & Stock
An Imprint of Wipf and Stock Publishers
199 W. 8th Ave., Suite 3
Eugene, OR 97401

www.wipfandstock.com

ISBN 13: 978-1-61097-752-4

The Word

For days, I tried to speak.
I opened my mouth but there were no words.
But then, as I sat down in surrendered silence to the void that engulfed me, words flowed like the freedom of water on a hidden brook while I gazed at something that mirrors the splendor of space and the present moment.

These words are not like the hollow theorems I read in factory-made books; nor are they similar to my ego-driven opinions.

They seem alive, innocent, *in*-spired.

They emanate from the unseen union of the poet and the Source.

They are the incarnated divine that satisfies the hungry and usher the seekers to eternal living.

They are not confined within the doctrinal margin of sacred texts.

Nor are they strictly bestowed to teachers, scientists or the ordained.

They abide even before I conceived them, flowing freely and bountifully from the realm of the formless.

They are preexistent.

These living logos nonetheless are not aspiring for veneration.

They are symbols that point to the infinite Reality that is boundless, timeless and ineffable.

The gospels describe a wise Teacher in days of old, as the Logos and the full expression of God.

But he himself said that he came to glorify the Father —the Source, the Sustainer, the Whole.

And so after spending many days in the gulf of painful silence where I saw neither images nor inscriptions, I was gradually awakened by the still small voice of living idioms.

And like poetry and music, it is starting to breathe life into my callous soul once more.

And thus I began to write . . .

Contents

Foreword by Robert Corin Morris *ix*

Preface xiii

Acknowledgments xix

one I Am Nowhere 1

two I Was A Homeowner 7

three I Was Homeless Inside a Home 21

four I Am Homeless 37

five I Am 50

six I Am Home Always Already 59

seven I, Others, and the Pan 70

Conclusion: I Am Not Ferdie Anymore 102

Epilogue 105

Bibliography 109

Foreword

Sometimes what seems, on the surface, an emotional breakdown is actually an existential *breakthrough* rising up from the wellsprings of health in the deep psyche. *Home, I Am* is a story of just such a personal transformation. I have been privileged to walk as a spiritual companion and advisor to Ferdinand Llenado through many of the inner and outer events described in this metaphorical and symbolic story of transition, crisis, soul-purification and transformation.

When Ferdie came to see me I sensed immediately that his soul was aching to grow beyond the forms of his "first spirituality," that charismatic fundamentalism which gave him shelter, security and, I believe, a genuine connection with the Spirit in his teen years. He found a spiritual home, a powerful role for his ego to build an identity around, and a channel to exercise his considerable gifts of intelligence and creativity. But, as a wise Bishop once said to me, the soul has different seasons as it grows toward God, and what may be best at one stage of our lives may need to be left behind as we go deeper into God, or as the great mystical writer Evelyn Underhill would say, Reality.

One of the dangers of religion, especially religions with rigid codes and strictures, is that we can hide from who we are by living out a fantasy of who we ought to be. This can result in an increasingly pretended piety rather than the personal transformation of heart and mind authentic spiritual traditions are intended to foster. As the depth psychologist C. G. Jung would put it, we get lost in our *persona,* the mask we show to the world and ourselves. We lose touch with other parts of our whole, complex Selves, especially those that don't conform to our religious ideals. They get buried in the basement, to use Ferdie's metaphor, and become tormenting Shadows.

The mask, however is likely to slip repeatedly, even crumble; or the Shadows (which contain both potential good and potential evil) shout louder, and we have to come to terms with the reality of who we are.

This can create the sort of "spiritual emergency" Dr. Llenado bears witness to in these pages.[1] For me as an ordained priest and spiritual director, the sign of its spiritual authenticity is the place the author's psyche came to rest, in the midst of his troubles: that is, the humble affirmation of his utterly common humanity, full of both giftedness and brokenness, possibility and limitation. Ferdie's journey from defensiveness to acceptance, from arrogance to humility, and from fear to peace is, indeed, a story of coming home to the native ground of human nature—a ground in which good seed can grow robustly.

This stripping off of illusions and pretentions, this return to the simple identity of "I am" is, indeed, a sort of reunion with the nakedness of Adam and Eve in the Garden before they, the symbols of our own human journey, set off on his journey of assumed knowledge, power and arrogance. The stripping is, however, only half the story.

1. See Grof, *Spiritual Emergency.*

In his nakedness and vulnerability, Ferdie was given a fresh, almost wordless experience of Reality. He *awakened* to the reality of his profound inter-connectedness with everything from the vastness of the cosmos to the suffering of the people around him. He awakened to a compassion for himself and others that had not been given room to grow. And he awakened to a sense of the whole cosmos as sacred, the dwelling place of Spirit, one of the most widespread spiritual themes of our age. I have witnessed others make this same journey; indeed, I have been led along it myself. And I believe countless thousands of others are on a similar path.

The world is involved in a great, transitional, spiritual crisis. As in pivotal times in the past, the "new wine" of the Spirit is poured into a world of old wineskins, some of which burst because they are too small for God's current transformational activity. New ways of understanding ancient traditions compete to be the spiritual future—among them the more contemplative approach God's presence in ordinary life Dr. Llenado has discovered.

My hope is that Ferdie's witness to the goodness and grace of God which pursued him and helped burst his fetters, both psychological and religious, will encourage others facing similar difficulties, giving them confidence that the Spirit can work in strange and mysterious ways to "write straight with crooked lines," as an old proverb so aptly puts it.

The Rev. Dr. Robert Corin Morris
Founder, Interweave Center for Wholistic Living

Preface

THIS BOOK is a short memoir of my journey through a depression that was mainly caused by existential crisis. During its severity, I developed the practice of reflective writing, in which I experienced a great extent of inner healing. In my journal entries, I noticed a constant emergence of imageries that represented actual events and thoughts. It seemed that the use of images was effective in revealing my deepest emotions that otherwise would remain hidden from other forms of therapy.

One of the symbols that contributed significantly to my recovery was homelessness. The dire state of losing a permanent place, and wandering the streets alone, meaningfully reflected my helpless emotional condition. I continued this way of journaling until I saw the potential of my story and writing method in helping others who are going through the same internal crisis. The result is this short and rather ambitious metaphorical memoir.

Due to its symbolic nature, it is important that readers are reminded of the book's lyrical and abstract approach. Lyrical, reflecting not just my own poetic temperament but also my cultural background as a Filipino preacher. Abstract because the main plot of homelessness, with the events and characters surrounding it, are fictional. To further complicate things, the line between factual information and figurative depiction are blurred in some sections. Lessons and messages are therefore implied or even allusively buried in the intricacy of the story. This approach resonates with parables and folklores found in mystical or sacred writings, including many of Jesus' teachings in the gospels.

It is not my intention to convey confusion or to make it to the list of literary forgers. Rather, in my experience of writing essays, constantly identifying the historical and differentiating it from the symbolic, interrupts the smooth flow of poetic narration. Also, I found it more therapeutic when my writing freely dances between the realm of fiction and facts. Thus, in this book, I prioritized artistry, therapy, and emotional connectivity with readers, over the demand of facts and prose. In today's vast exploration of post-postmodern literature, this memoir can be a valuable contribution to emerging autobiographical writing.

Furthermore, the use of metaphor is not a strategy for hiding my fairly simple life. My story is not extraordinary, but it's not boring either, and I have no plan of masking it with dramas and anecdotes to appear interesting. Put another way, this metaphorical memoir is an attempt to convey reality through the concept of allegorical painting, except I used words instead of paints and brushes.

However, readers may find it helpful that I identified some of the facts that are embedded in this symbolic narrative. Below is a short description of the personal data I used in this book:

> I spent the last twenty years of my life as a pastor. The first half, I served in the Philippines, and the second half in the United States. During these years, I also earned two master's degrees and a doctorate. More than a year ago, the depression

that I was battling with for years plummeted into a serious nervous breakdown. After being hospitalized for a few days, I took a leave of absence from the ministry. It was during this period of disability and recovery that I started to write. Presently, I am a stay-at-home dad, which I now know as the most gratifying and meaningful opportunity someone could ever have. Moreover, the experience of being home helped me to internalize life in the concept of architectural design.

Another important theme that may need explanation is my constant usage of the first person, *I am*. I-am-ness is an essential theory in this book due to its significant role in restoring my emotional stability. When existential crisis left me with critical anxiety disorder, it was the affirmation of my beingness—through a silent confession of who I am— that slowly reconstructed my belief system. Furthermore, some readers can also attest that I-am-ness coincides with substantial philosophical, psychological, and mystical traditions. The high emphasis on I-am-ness therefore is non-narcissistic, but rather a testimony to my recent spiritual experience.

There are at least four other things that are in need of explanation. First, it will be evident to readers how twenty years of preaching affected my pattern of writing. Alliterating the chapters, key sections, and title (if you haven't notice yet) was just too tempting for me to resist. It was also fun to build intensity in some sections through rhythmic patterns and repetitious phrase; a homiletical habit I developed over the years. Most importantly, some components of the plot allude to biblical events and languages. To sound preachy is far from my intention. But for now, it seems that the most effective way I can write is through sermonic discourse.

Second, people of all trades may notice in their reading that I am not a handyman. To say the least, my wife gets scared every time I carry a wrench around the house. But through personal research and inquiry, I gained a small knowledge of carpentry and architecture, which was enough for the parts I needed to expand through metaphor. However, if there is information mentioned in this book that readers may find architecturally inaccurate, I sincerely apologize.

Third, I do not imply that reflective writing is applicable to all cases of depression. There are various choices of behavioral and group therapy that may be more compatible with other contexts. Mine is only but a hope that somehow my story, my method of writing, and my learning in this spiritual journey, be an inspiration for the emotionally homeless to find their way home.

Last, there are at least two sections in the concluding chapter that are more descriptive of my spiritual goals rather than describing the past or present: portions of the *I am* affirmation; and the chapter where I went to another shack to help someone who was going through a similar crisis. These scenes can represent my envisioned next step toward further recovery and a future ministry.

And so, this is for you: you who gave it all serving others but found yourself by the wayside worn-out and alone; you who quit church, or society, or school, or self, or home; you who are misunderstood because your belief system is expanding; you who are going through a midlife crisis of identity and meaning; you who seek success but found real solace in silence; you who are justifiably angry; you who because of pain can only converse in arts, songs, or metaphors; you who feel homeless, emotionally, psychologically, spiritually; this is for you, you are the *I am* who is already and eternally home.

Acknowledgments

My deepest appreciations go to the people who helped and inspired me to write this book.

To the United Methodist Church, for giving me a place of ministry and fellowship;

To Lynn Russo Whylly, for helping me edit the early chapters of my book;

To Robert Corin Morris, for being a tireless mentor and a faithful friend;

To my mom, my dad, my brothers, and my sisters for constantly supporting me in prayer, love, and finances;

To my wife, Louie and our three children, Jedidiah, Hiram, and Theo Jonas, for being my inspiration, my healing, and my home.

one

I Am Nowhere

I AM nowhere: no home, no hope, and nearly no heartbeat. But still, they found me. It's now six days since this standoff began. I am surrounded by five ancient Shadows and the only thing delaying my death is the train's thick alloy wall that is reinforced by intersected steel strap.

I am worn out. Powerless. Trapped.

The old metal shack that had sheltered me is now beaten badly. The air is already filled with a vile stench. Despair is gathering with renewed force. I swallowed my last fluid. I used my last ploy. I emptied my last prayer pot. It's just a matter of time.

As I sat motionless on a moldy rubber floor, I thought of death and how funny God is for choosing this place as my private mausoleum. I smiled at the absurdity of such thought.

"This isn't so bad," I said to myself.

This strange feeling made me realize, however, that I am less afraid, and probably more insane. I decided to write ... words that could probably be my last.

I am nowhere—writing from a scrapped home, an abandoned railway carriage, forgotten. For a few days this place was a home. From where I am slumped, I can see the austerity of the night sky through a small crack in the roof.

The young bamboo plant that sprouted in the middle of this dark space is still here—steady, tender, and abiding since day one.

The sound of drilling and excavating that comes from an underground mining area is now starting to fade. The miners told me the other day that they already extracted all the minerals and coals, and they are now in the process of burying the shaft . . . which reminded me of my impending death and my eventual burial place.

Really, it's not that bad. The stench of dead lab rats from a nearby landfill represents the foul smell of death. The dehydrated weeds on the wall embody the dry flowers you see on gravestones. The graffiti tells me that I'm not the first one who died here. But the most humorous part in this mental satire is the fact that I used to bury people. I was a pastor, and yes I can conduct my own funeral!

In addition, I was a homeowner for twenty remarkable years. The house was more than residential. It was an oasis of meaning, a divine plethora, a sacred space where my soul experienced rest. It was an open sanctuary where visitors were served with nourishment and healing balms. It was a felt presence in the religious community I was living with.

A few years ago, our town meetings started to accommodate circuit riders—clerics and lecturers who rode on horseback to speak from one place to another. Remodeling designs and alternative architectures were presented in eloquence and impressive slideshows by young silver-tongued entrepreneurs.

One of them stood out prominently and was always given a celebrity welcome. An attractive young man dressed in hipster attire, he bedazzled listeners with Neverland rhetoric. He used new jargons like organic, emergent, generous orthodoxy, neomonastic, and post-*everything*, to describe a new age of homeownership. They called him Peter Pan. I bought his books and hung in my room pictures of his model houses. My restlessness grew as I seriously absorbed this growing trend.

While developing suspicion with the credibility of my design, unforeseen flaws behind the paint and classic moldings began appearing one after another. The increasing number of cracks on the floor revealed a defective structural foundation. Quick fixes and denial proved valuable at first. But the demands of maintenance mode just got pointless. I slowly noticed that appearances do not motivate me anymore. Growth ceased its previous role as stimulant. Compassion fatigue caught up and dragged me by the wayside a few times.

After a while, I became cynical with the larger community—the institutional church in the midst of a broken humanity. I was embarrassed with my missiology degree that got drained of missional spirit. I got burdened with those heavy clerical robes and charismatic homilies. I was developing a solomonic syndrome of utter meaninglessness. But I was too proud to ask for help and too paranoid to open the door to sympathetic friends.

The soul searching became brutal. I already noticed the stupidity of the questions and where they were headed. But I had already lost control, or I believed I did. And as if it was the last detonating cord to arm a huge pack of TNT, I was ready to implode.

I developed a destructive rage. Blinded by the same light that awakened me, I became an angry judge. I conducted a drab court proceeding that concluded with a seemingly irreversible verdict: all is vanity. Afterward, I gave the house a bloody pounding. After an all-night demolition, I stood panting and weeping in the midst of my own wreckage, where once stood a stable beautiful home.

I am now homeless: condemned by my own conscience; lost in the oblivion of depression.

People started to speculate why I got depressed. "Church work got too much for him," they said. To some reasonable extent yes, pastoral work is strenuous. But I am not a wishy-washy undependable person. I have my small share of trophies and credentials on the wall of personal achievement to prove it.

I know how to run. I've been through battlefields. I've sailed through dark storms and came out with bruises and badges. At the age of 19, I started a church while finishing up college. At 22, I was a recognized speaker in conferences, camps, and churches. I went to places where others would not go as a revivalist and a missionary. I adapted to a life of asceticism and turned terribly pale from excessive fasting. I received a doctoral diploma and two master's degrees. From an average teen in an unknown third world barrio, I was single-handedly able to have a ministerial career in the U.S. At a young age, I learned the art of consistency, stability, and focus.

But tell me, when the ideological foundation is shaken, how will a nation proceed? How can great cities endure with polluted wall streets and waterways? When a home becomes hades, where will the children go? What is philosophy with dead Emersons? Science without aviators? Death with no promise of a resurrection?

When my fabric of meaning withered, how was I supposed to carry on? What is the point of breathing when my existence was uncertain? How can I continue preaching faith if my malignant disease was unbelief? What is church growth then? What is a three-point exegetical sermon? What is a doctrinal treatise? What is an eighteenth-century steeple? What is a doctoral dissertation? What are crowns, bank accounts, plaques of recognition? The questions went on while the answers dried up.

Then about two weeks ago, I was brought to a behavioral hospital due to severe depression. I stayed there for six days.

I am out now but still paralyzed. I am afraid to build a new home; to make the same mistake; to reprocess the old blueprint. A second meltdown will be unbearable. And so as I sit naked in the corroded corner of this carriage, I am strangely comforted by the condition of my incompetence. My disability can be a sound justification for laziness and procrastination. Is it possible that this homelessness is the beginning of an unconscious reconstruction of a peculiar house? One that is worse than before? One that is built like a dark infirmary designed to certify indolence and admit me as a spiritual refugee? Is my homelessness starting to become an unconscious home? Dark? Haunted? Built by the same depression that had destroyed my first home?

I am nowhere or now here—in this undesirable "nowness" and unknown "hereness."

It's now quiet outside. Not the kind that emits peace. But like a chilling stillness before a storm; or like an ambush hiding behind a safe valley. Time is reaching its culmination and it seems that the final phase of my life confined me with one ability left—to write. I am now seated nearer the young bamboo tree. I just touched the leaves again. It is still fresh, green, and calming. It reminded me of home.

two

I Was a Homeowner

I WAS always fascinated with knowledge: space exploration, the sub-atomic realm, human anatomy, and some odd ensembles of popular sciences. But somehow, the path of spirituality captivated me more: mystery, shared ecstasy, oracles, glossolalia, and the ironic pleasure of asceticism.

Sadly, the form of spiritual path that was offered where I used to live was covered with deep-rooted fundamentalism. It taught me how to label other houses as haunted or demonic. The walls that sheltered me also estranged me from fields of knowledge that point to the same reality I was seeking. Obviously, my vision was so programmed to read dualistically back then that I could not see the world in whole. All I could see were separate houses and an audacious need to have my own.

Founded not in academic thoughts but mostly upon mystical knowledge, I slowly constructed my dream house. Eventually, I was classified with the young entrepreneurs who enjoyed homeownership in the religious neighborhood.

Yes, many years ago I was a homeowner. I remember quite richly the smell of old books in the foyer; the laughter shared among visiting friends; the dripping of water in the miniature falls; the restful nights in a secured room; the fragrance of incense; and the unseen presence that pervades in that divine space.

It is so tempting to look back through the marks of the present scars. But I hope I can reminisce the past without reliving too much of the pain.

THE EARLY CONSTRUCTION

The house that I once owned was huge and beautiful. The walls were designed with classic craftsmanship and the ceiling with symmetrical ornamentation. The interior was filled with contemporary furniture and multimedia accessories, where one's craving for hi-tech simulation will certainly be satisfied.

I started building this house when I was fourteen. At a young age, I realized that I was not meant to live in my parents' house for long.

I cannot live a life of purpose with an inherited faith.

I cannot find my soul by staring at a mainline creed.

I cannot learn a new language listening to fixed principles.

So I went outside the box, the teenage norm, the institution, the menagerie, the sacred parental blessing. I left my childhood home.

As I tread the exciting but dark alleys of freedom, the image of the house I once knew gradually faded. I was terrified. But my naïve idealism reminded me that this is my fate. So I continued walking about two inches above the pavement with a divine smirk.

One day, my attention was caught by some loud music coming from a parade that led to a brightly lit house. It was a Pentecostal church. Loud! They were loud. They sang loud. They prayed loud. I've never seen worshippers look so constipated during silent prayer. But it was not the "loud" that attracted me to them. It was the live wire in their songs that defibrillated my heart. It was the authenticity that radiated on the face of their dreamers. It was their jagged gospel that pierced my intellect, pouring out service and passion. It was their yieldedness to the mystery they could not convey—manifesting into the ecstasy of speaking in tongues.

Like the peaceful flow that happens in silence, they rest through divine utterances. Like a poet holding a restless pen, they verbalized their inspirations. I was drawn to that light like a wanderer saved from a heavy blizzard. In that house, I drank the wine. I caught the fire. I saw a glimpse of the divine. I started to understand, to preach, and to write. I engaged in the miraculous, asserting my authority in demonic strongholds. I challenged policies, traditions, powers, wearing the "thus saith the Lord" garb. I gained a lot of respect and loads of opponents.

I overheard comments that I was more pentecostal than those I mimic. I took them as more than sycophantic compliments. They became my identity, my goal, segments of the blueprint. From a potential overnighter, I assimilated in the family as the tightly-laced child. I learned to speak the newest spiritual jargon, adapted the imperative posture, embodied the heroic, and delivered the most pompous homilies that made a tongue-talking crowd speechless.

Furthermore, my young psyche's need for stability was supplied by dogmatism. Spiritual infilling—with the initial evidence of tongue talking—quenched my thirst for the esoteric. Their graphic description of hell transformed my introvertism into a messianic personage who invades hell's gate to rescue the condemned.

My theology was accurate.

My mandate was urgent.

My sense of meaning was strong.

Soon after, I was a model resident in this swiftly expanding house of the charismatic.

But tagging along with this blissful phase of my journey was a nagging voice that kept me awake at night: raising questions that made some Sundays a dreaded day to wait for; showing loopholes in dogmatism that once covered my nakedness. So I asked my teachers how to silence the internal heretic with sharp apologetics. With them, I learned steadiness quite well . . . and more.

I also learned how inconsistencies can be patched with the miraculous; or how spiritual music can restrain my need to explore the unorthodox and alternatives. Brick by brick, I built citadels to both define and defend my identity. The stronger my fundamentalism was, the safer. The deeper the piety was, the holier.

After a while however, I got tired of the shows, the claims, and the hallelujahs. I peeked through the windows and saw wisdom in balanced architectures. As I continued to study other home designs, the walls I built inside my hostess' house metamorphosed into a separate structure—I was gradually leaving the home that first sheltered me.

I was ready to build my own.

Leaving the herd and building a distinctive identity was both daring and deranged. But I was determined to no longer replicate the iconic houses around me. I have learned to fuse evangelicalism, pentecostalism, and a small touch of liberalism in one structural design. The blueprint was complex. The flavor was unique. The innovation was a risk. But it was this same pungency that made me romantically curious.

From excavation to soil treatment, from plumbing to flooring, and from painting to landscaping, the house was skillfully and slowly built. It was my creation, my worldview, my passion, my aesthetic, my purpose, my identity. It was my home.

I was committed to complete this noble project. A dream house built upon the principle of balance: between energy and word, power and reason, innovation and tradition, the prophetic and the academia, the pious and the political, sin and poverty, conversions and social change. At first I gained more approval, entered more territories, crossed more denominational borders. Exhibiting wisdom and originality in a soft voice, I secured respect and recognition. I was known as the open-minded, balanced, model home. I was building some high walls.

It seems however that the higher I built, the higher the expectations. And I will soon find out that expectations can be lethal to one's soul. They can cause serious harm.

They can distract the single-minded.

They can pollute intentions.

They can impede a noble journey.

They can damage a fine abode.

Instead of the house I want, I can, I was becoming, I was developing a habit of meeting expectations.

I removed a nativity scene from the backyard to avoid upsetting some neighbors. I rearranged the furniture to accommodate more visitors. I hung portraits of people I needed to flatter. I did general clean-up on Saturdays to prepare the house for the next day. I learned some tools of quick fixes: spackles, fresheners, curtains, sealants, and the almighty duct tape.

There were cliffhanger episodes that pushed me to near breakdown. Ironically, they were also lifesavers. When parts of the house were showing signs of serious abrasions, the lifestyle of pleasing others was a good energy source. But some expectations were exhausting at times—the forced smile on a dreary Sunday morning; the healing services I led while fighting my own flu; the strenuous nod to a self-absorbed counselee; the calm reply when an outburst seemed pretty sensible; and canned sermons delivered pompously to movers and spectators.

These actions were not necessarily inauthentic. Most of them were done with good intentions—to rescue, to reconcile, to pacify, to please. It is called civility, accountability, and empowering others. I was aware, however, that energies gained from meeting expectations would not last. They could not be used for an extended period and for most of life's challenges.

In time, I needed to revive the inner well.

I needed to reignite the spiritual fire.

I needed to renovate the house.

To do this, I needed to close the doors for a period of makeover.

But opportunities were scarce. People kept coming in. Demands were expanding. Expectations were building up.

So I continued receiving guests while the inner layer of the house was rotting within its well-garlanded sheathings.

Thus, the joy of every success was accompanied by fear—fear that people will see through my eyes the sadness behind the sparkle, the guilt behind piety, and the emptiness behind the pretenses.

And I was right. After a while, my fears came true (or maybe this paranoia just worsened). The angst was leaking out. The masks were wearing out. The frightening realities became more apparent—I could not please all, I should not save all, and I would not be all that people expected me to be.

I am not trying to sound naïve. I know the concept of realism. I memorized the biblical references. I preached the "all have fallen short" sermons on countless Sundays. It's a different story, however, when one's idealism and the qualms that follow it are deeply rooted in one's faith and meaning. The season of crisis can be deadly.

Unexpectedly, my pretenses and postures proved favorable though. The news about my vibrant house reached my superiors. They heard me speak. They read my resume. They came and conducted a house assessment. It was concluded that I was the ideal candidate for a distinctive mission—to design and build a new home. The project was called "house-start."

It was a career risk, and at the same time, the only chance left open for me to escape the poisonous paranoia and boredom I was experiencing inside this freakish home. You know, a new environment, a fresh start, a clean slate. In building another house, I thought I could heal my own. With full knowledge of the risk and a strong hope for heaven's blessing, I accepted the job. Little did I know that this decision would be the trigger point of a serious breakdown and the missionfield, well, my graveyard.

My home takes many names.

Sometimes I call it fundamentalism.

Sometimes, pastoral work.

Sometimes it's my own piety.

It was my identity, my meaning, my purpose, my dwelling place.

All of us have one or more homes, calling them in different names: power, tribe, expertise, story, land, reputation, fascination, wealth, policy, romance, disability, religion, culture, or aesthetics. However we label it, they serve as our security, significance, and way of life. Although each is designed differently according to our genetic and cultural makeup, all are meant to evolve, expand, and embrace wider. There are seasons in this growth process that are unbearably shattering—aggravated by its isolating nature.

But before I recount the tragedy part, a quick tour will give readers a better context of my eventual homelessness. The tour is described in present tense as if readers will go back in time with me when I still owned a delightful and impressive home.

Welcome. Please come in.

THE TOUR

There is little elegance with the exterior. The front window is a classic double-hung sash that is covered with opaque white curtains. A wooden front door painted with bluish red and topped with bow glass creates a churchy appearance—always inviting, and never shut on weekends. There is no lawn though, only a ground level porch that is extended around the right wing window.

As you enter the house, you are warmly greeted by a small foyer that leads to a spacious living room. The floor is bamboo hardwood, overarched by a cathedral ceiling. The walls are solid concrete embellished with classy carvings and stained glass murals.

The furniture is a strange mix of old Victorian savor and modern Asian plainness (if that is even conceivable). This combination gained both praise and derogatory emails. In addition to this congestion are built-in theater gadgets with the latest hi-fi madness. But overall, it's a fine interior center.

There is a huge antique rock at the heart of the open space where calm water flows constantly. Many visitors testified to the therapeutic effect of this interior waterfall.

There are four rooms that are separated by portable partitions. On certain occasions, the rooms are merged to create a bigger space. But they mostly function in their own intricate personages.

The Servant Room

In this room I wear a robe, a big silver cross, and an incessant smile. I carry a ritual manual, a traveler communion set, and a thick study bible. Most people who I encountered in this space don't know my name. I am only referred to as a designation—reverend, clergy, preacher. But it is within this hallowed space where souls are healed, the confused are counseled, and the wayward finds a home. There is also a 24-hour hotline and an in-home service option. The room is well lit. The windows are wide open. The furniture is spotless. There is no bed but only a large number of stackable chairs.

Behind the pulpit, I am pompously loud. Facing a counselee, I am soft and grace-packed. In board meetings, I am a quiet negotiator. For my superiors, I am a front seat asset. To fluctuating parishioners, I am their seasonal entertainer. To the faithful, I am like a revered effigy.

The walls in this room are covered in plaques, some deserving of the showcase, and some just to cover the cracks and delaminated paints. A portion of the ceiling is sunroof while the rest are made with acoustic ceiling tiles. The room is twenty years old and I'm only in my late-thirties.

In this room, I am a pastor.

The Mystic Room

It's dark but not dreary. The light from beeswax candles pervades the room with unseen ripples of serenity. In this room, I usually wear a plain linen ephod and, at desperate times, I wear sackcloth. I kneel in front of a burnt altar where I usually perform sacrificial offerings. Traces of blood are still evident around the holy chancel where I slew teen indulgences during my early years of asceticism. The flame from the altar seems like tongues of fire where spontaneous utterances are heard. At times, the flame is so strong that it harmed the few I allowed to enter the room. These two elements: the quiet ripple and the scorching flame represent the mystic that I am.

The Thinker Room

The door and windows are tightly shut. I seldom allow visitors to come in because I want the fixtures and ornaments to stay tidy and linear. I have a small collection of books that are shelved thematically: theological, philosophical, and spiritual. From theories of inerrancy to levels of christologies; from the charismatics' pneuma to strange eschatologies; from classical exegesis to contextual theology; from Luther to Tillich; from Barth to Zacharias; from Finney to Kuhlman; from Aldersgate to Azusa Street. It sounds extensive, but it's not. My textbooks are carefully canonized. My shelves have a high censorship, defined by fundamentalism. Here, I am like a flirtatious old guard—audacious with spiritual ecstasy, but a curator of ancient creeds.

Later on, it will be evident how this room started to break down. Due perhaps to a lack of usage and sentimental loyalty to its preservation, I was not able to repair the damages and upgrade the appliances.

A Room Called, Well, Ferdie

The room is small. The paint is dull gray. Some of the fixtures are extinct. The space is a disappointing austerity to my colleagues. I am the youngest of five siblings, yet I walk the gray-haired life. I am the obedient child that did not use my "prodigal license." I am the army cadet, the law-abiding local, and the bona fide weirdo.

As narrated earlier, I experienced a chronic boredom with meeting expectations. Thus, I began hitchhiking with Pentecostal caravans. They themselves encouraged me to consider some serious remodeling and a minor expansion of the back wall. And I did.

Although the drama I caused can take home some Oscar statuettes, the spur and disenchantment were only temporary. Soon, I was the darling of both players and onlookers. I was the model student that turned deviant, but was later hailed as a protagonist.

As years go by however, this room became smaller while the other rooms expanded. As the parish grew, close friends were lessened. As the other rooms evolved, people began to forget my name.

Furthermore, I also became an eccentric medley of monotony and deviation: methodical in personal piety but unorthodox in goal-setting; the old-fashioned soul with an unrestrained vitality of a juvenile.

The Attic

For years, I testified that I had already burned my attic. It was not a deliberate lie. I believed in the same stubborn doctrine myself. In this town, to think otherwise is almost blasphemy. Because it was in the attic where Lucifer became an adversary, it is in the attic where haughtiness have built clever snares to lurk the unsuspecting... we thought.

It angered us.

And so, a few years ago, we declared war on the devil's war. We designed strategies. We recruited fanatics. We invested in spiritual ammunitions. The fight was on. It was spiritual warfare at daylight.

After weeks of intense combat, the dust settled, the houses were visible again. Some homeowners hung banners and laurels on their porch. To some, it became part of their resume—"attic-free." To others, it gave them a calling—"attic–removal ministry." The principle was soon used as a measurement of spiritual attainment, at least in my neighborhood.

It was only later that I realized how pathetic and stupid the claim was, because the more I denied my attic's existence, the more it became visible to the wise around me. The more I tried to lock it, the more the door expanded. The passionate I grew to get rid of it, the longer I spent time inside it. The angrier I got with it, the more it defined my ambitions. The fire I used to burn it became part of its character—upsettingly bright and fervent. It was like trying to control a smart teleportation machine from inside it—the more you push buttons, the more it moves you elsewhere.

This attic is called Ego.

This is by far the most enigmatic room in the house. The depression that I will experience later will give an aching awareness that this allegedly condemned attic called Ego was never really torn down. It is not only intact, it also expanded its control of the house cunningly: the enthusiasm that is powered by messianic complex; indigenization that turned ethnocentric; spirituality fortified by stiff calvinism; judgment as an occasional sleeping aid; the inflated addenda in my resume; and my annoying preachy accent.

So, here we are inside the most misconstrued floor of my home. The trophies and plaques are still in place. The laminated diplomas are hanging close to my small study carrel. The clippings, sketches, and all those clever multicolored sticky notes are held firmly in the strategy board. They all represent my messianic goals, my exclusivism, and my religious chivalry.

Finally, there in an elevated area of the flooring is an oil canvas self-portrait, painted with short brush strokes.

The A-basement

The atmosphere is dark, unlike the brightly lighted attic. It is not just the absence of light, it is the presence of evil. If the attic is a pseudo-heaven, the basement is the bottomless pit. It is the room where my own awareness doesn't enter. I'll rather address it as a separate entity than recognize it as part of my home. It is a creepy ghost town, a corpse among vultures, a lair of demons.

Basements are meant to be exorcised, not understood. They are better hidden than inhabited; undiagnosed than treated; unspoken in conversations, like those repressed emotions. Although the ugly image is kept unseen beneath, the stench of dampness and decay will climb up at times and ruin my day. If I have guests, I'll tell them I just fried some exotic food or just blame it on the neighbors.

You are in my basement. Its shade is getting more uncontainable, as you can sense. Its power is starting to crawl up to the main floor. Let's get out of here. I hope the dampness was not too foul to suffocate you.

This concludes the tour. I know it was not that entertaining, but I think it is an effective framework for understanding the succeeding chapters because, from here on out, the tone of my writing will get heavier as the progression of the events get darker.

three

I Was Homeless Inside a Home

A BEACH house, a corner office, or a shortcut to stardom; a Casanova, a prom queen, or a dream vacation; a PhD, a vindication, a dramatic ending, heroism; globalization, a medical breakthrough, the unexplored cosmos, or the uncharted realm of the abyssal zone; healing, reconciliation, birth, death, and freedom. Some are labeled as desires, some worldviews, some quests, some answers, and others as meaning. They create aspirations, awaken compassion, provide stability, write stories, affirm our humanity, and enrich our existence. We use sciences to structure them, cultures to cultivate them, politics to govern them, and poetry to describe them.

In my life journey, I mostly look at them in metaphors. I guess my aesthetic lenses are more dominant than my other genes. And as I recollect this crisis episode, I see and experienced it through the image and sensation of home and homelessness. As expressed earlier, I was once a homeowner. The promises attached to homeownership were true—meaning, identity, contentment, certainty. But what the academician, the conventional scientist, the top dog vicar, the Hollywood icon, or the Wall Street players did not tell us is the temporal phase of homeownership.

Meaning, I think houses should not stay in the same form through their lifespan. They are wired for periodic renovations. Resisting their design for growth can result in pain and disparity. Ignoring their need for change can lead to obstinacy and pride. When my doctrinal axioms were threatened, I applied good apologetics to reinforce the wall. The nastier the debate, the stronger I got. The more discouraging the situation, the longer I fasted. The faultier the heresy, the louder I preached. I honestly thought I was doing the flock under my roof a favor . . . and to some extent, maybe I was.

But it became necessary later on, that in order for me to upgrade the security of my home, I would need to be more critical of others. I was later charged with religious unpleasantness and was found guilty by many. After years of using this approach, I started to be critical of myself.

It was at this time that I began to harbor Shadows in the basement. I was not fully aware of who they were and how to deal with them. So I tried to do what I was good at— perform self-exorcism sessions when no one was around. There were days when I was convinced that I scoured the basement clean. Then the stench and creepy noises came back—a bit stronger and vociferous.

I cannot name most of them. But the loudest and more devious, I was able to identify.

ABSURD

Of all the spiritual warfare I engaged with, the presence of the Absurd upstaged all of my foes. Like an insatiable cancer, it devoured my hollow organs. It preyed on me like a skillful predator. The deriding grin as it sat silently in the pew disarmed many of my homilies. It impersonated my conscience as it whispered, meaningless.

Amity, meaningless.

Glory, meaningless.

Credence, meaningless.

The Absurd continued. It clouded my vision so I could see its enormous shade covering the entirety of existence, including mine: this tedious rat race we call work-life; empty rituals I do before dead parishioners; melancholia in the early stage of boredom; the migrant's illusion of greener pastures; the blind faith of truth claims; the finiteness we can never crack; the endless mystery that will not yield; the genocides we are all guilty of not halting; the evil that we seem to portray as omnipotent; and the inevitable fangs of death.

Like a wounded hero in a bad Hollywood film, I fell helpless in the grip of this unrelenting demon.

I met with heroes and victims of the past who battled with the same adversary. Albert Camus showed me how to flip coins tauntingly in the dark while describing the paradox of being. I followed him and mocked the Absurd for a while, but sarcasm is just not my style.

Kierkegaard praised the strong subjectivity I developed over the years and encouraged me to deepen my doubt. He argued that I should trust doubt as an enhancer of faith. To further complicate the irony, the more I believed that God would help my unbelief, the more I doubted, and thus the more I grew my faith.

Then there were neurotics like Nietzsche. What a character and what atrocity. He came in my house blasting off his shotgun at everything that depicted morality, hierarchy and spirituality. He tried to justify his actions by declaring his infamous claim, "God is dead." After accusing him of trespassing, we sat down and discussed how his ideas paved the way for postmodern thinkers like Sartre, Foucault, or Derrida—which at that time I was starting to read. I listened for a while and then politely asked him to leave.

They were short meetings, but they were enough for them to dispense their views and viruses. And because of the already spreading corrosion in the house and my pride of avoiding professional help, I now question whether my exposure to complicated thinkers was more harm than help.

After a few weeks, the Absurd secured a dark lair in the center of my fascination. My sincere thirst for knowledge was gradually possessed by sick uncontrollable thoughts. Like the tempter's strategy to lure Jesus off the cliff, I was drawn to come nearer the edge of sanity so I could finally behold the face of meaning. But unlike the gospel story, I yielded to the invitation and was swallowed helplessly in the depths of dire uncertainties.

AUTHENTIC

I've seen a lot of houses and lived in some of them. But the houses of religious fanatics charmed me most. In their porch hung large banners with bold words that claimed authenticity. Some of them traveled from one town to another knocking on doors. With them was a ghostly figure that emanated a captivating presence—the Authentic. One day, I saw them passing by my street and I eagerly followed. They were headed to a brightly lit house by the hill. It was a Pentecostal church. The place was packed with rhetoric and symbols that claim the presence and infilling of the Authentic. I was hooked. Although there were some obvious displays of hyperbole, they were not enough to discourage my novice wonder.

As I mentioned earlier, when I was ready to build my own house, I borrowed some of their ideas. I was unaware back then that pure authenticity is not just uncopyable but is also unrealistic. Signs of unsteadiness soon became evident. Corrosion appeared on hidden corners. But no one was able to convince me back then that there were flaws in the blueprint, nor that the proposed materials were substandard. I always thought then that it was because I had not prayed enough, I had not performed enough, and I had not produced enough.

And so, after every event of failure, I ran the race faster, beat the tithing benchmark harder, or pushed the level of abstinence to disturbing severity. As far as I can remember, I was sincerely aiming for the Authentic—holiness, selflessness, Christlikeness. And in spite of some disturbances I created, the religious neighborhood seemed to agree that my intentions were pure. I was the prophet, the prototype, the pioneer of spiritual renewal and authentic lifestyle in my community.

But just like many endeavors that started with noble goals, the spirit behind the law later withered; truth-claims deprioritized meekness; charity was overshadowed by the demands for signs and wonders. While I stayed faithful to external religion, my internal source was slowly drying up. The pressing voice that absolute authenticity is a broader highway rather than a narrow and straight path was getting louder. But the decreasing likelihood of attaining this sinless state that I got so obsessed with was very difficult to swallow. Moreover, the disappointment was just the start of other more damaging behaviors that followed.

First, my selfless quest for the Authentic was mechanically turning into dead legalism. Only a few in my inner circle noticed. But a small gossip can spread so harmfully that it would surely dishearten the many whom I rescued out of spiritual homelessness. I have no choice. I have to be responsible for this collective hope I created, that the Authentic is real and attainable. And so I adapted the ultimate paradox: faking authenticity with authentic intentions—safeguarding the believers from backsliding and shielding the gospel from criticism. Consequently, pastoral care became automated, sermons got more condemning, and my campaign for spiritual revival turned self-righteous.

After some time however, my defenses slowly gave in. Again, I tried exploring the middle path to apply balance in my ministry. But because of my deep orientation with "either-or" thinking, I found myself tilting to the opposite extreme—persuadable, complacent, lenient, and exposed. I felt justified with this behavior because I was somewhat recompensing from the damages I caused while intoxicated with pharisaic spirits, again vindicated by good intentions—to make amends with loved ones I neglected, church people I hurt, and heresy I started. This too was an attempt to seek the Authentic.

Furthermore, my exposures with remodeling designs made me suspicious of everything conventional—from the house's touch of colonial architecture to its outmoded wood carvings; from its exotic hardwood to the walls' classic brass paint; from its semi-Victorian interior to its rustic metal roofing.

I started to question their durability and aesthetics. Not long after that, I tested the deconstruction theory in small segments of the house. I bought a heavy double-faced sledgehammer and tore up a few walls to create open spaces. I brought down some oil paintings and replaced them with *trompe l'oeil* and virtual arts to convey complexities and the illusion of depth. I collected ornaments from various cultures and arranged them eclectically in each room. I experimented with non-orthogonal angles and unconventional surfaces, but I was too inexperienced with cutting-edge tools so I was only able to finish a few items out of them.

Then came the aftereffect: post-construction mess, damaged pipes, angry neighbors, eye rashes, broken tools, and an almost comical combination of colonial, oriental, and surreal postmodern hues. At first the results were amusing, then promising, and then I saw a house made of failure—my lame attempts to experience the Authentic. I was regretful of the past, plagued by the present facts, and anxious of impending uncertainties.

However, it was also a season of revelation. The deconstruction tools I used backfired and dissected my intention. It unveiled the real face of the Authentic. It was a devious Shadow—a con-artist, a wolf in a shepherd's robe, a vile apparition. It took my innocent passion for authenticity and turned it into a self-consuming obsession. It lured me to search for the immaculate in priestly bylaws. It created a simulation of blissful Zion when I was in a trance with fellow fanatics. It made me hope for the unattainable—create a spotless mansion "as it is created in heaven." I was heroic. I was dramatic. I was a fireball.

My goal was lofty and so my fall was dreadful.

From that fall the same Shadow came, picked me up and encouraged me to romanticize my bitterness.

"This is your test, your destiny, the valley that leads to the flipside but perfect highland," it whispered.

And so this Shadow ushered me to develop new behaviors: weakness to exhibit meekness, leniency to preserve unity, ballots to avoid conflict, unconditional pleasantness to meet fixed expectations. Gradually, I learned the skill of going through the motions. Survival replaced significance. Spiritual passion turned into impersonal career. It was a hopeless shot to experience authenticity.

After this upsetting discovery, I wished for the Shadow to go away. I tried exorcism, but it just ignored my hollering. I begged for it to go but it just taunted my lameness. Then it became so parasitic that it embedded itself in some parts of the house. In some rooms, it was impossible to distinguish the Shadow from the walls, flooring, and furniture. I had one option left: tear down the house with it and then rebuild. It was suicidal, and as I mentioned earlier, I took the risk, and died.

ANGER

I first noticed the problem when the heating system exhibited erratic behavior and the wood stove made strange noises in the dead of the night. I developed this homemade wood-powered device when I was still young and impulsive. It was designed to generate electricity by feeding it constant firewood—charcoal, sawdust, logs. Fuel supply was never an issue when exorcism was still in my resume. Spiritual drills taught me how to gather up abhorrence toward Satan so that the stove was always given enough fuel to produce its share of juice.

The fuel was anger and the energy created was my passion for spiritual warfare. Again, it was not my sole source of momentum. But it was so powerful that there were days that it could charge the whole house with all the missional and pastoral fervor I needed for a dynamic ministry performance.

But when my vision of the otherworldly started to fade, Satan, the focus of my anger, faded out with it. There was no more target. There was no need for battlefields. The war in the basement was over. Consequently, the fuel supply lessened, the stove malfunctioned, the voltage dropped to a minimal capacity, until it nearly died. Could it be that part of my former meaning was defined by my nemesis? That my mission was advancing at a similar rate with how I interpret the Devil's pace—but toward the opposite trajectory? For a while, the warfare rhetoric softened while lethargy occupied some sections of the house.

Evangelism lost its urgency.

Eschaton plummeted from my narrative priority chart.

After a few years the fire reignited. The oven restarted. There was fuel again. But strangely, almost no energy was emitted. There was only this creepy noise from the basement, which I thought was caused by the busted machine. Then the shocking discovery—the stove metamorphosed into a vicious Shadow. Anger evolved from a coal component to a sycophantic entity that developed an ability to possess other mass. This strange mutation gave birth to the third Shadow which I simply called Anger. Moreover, it identified new enemies.

First, I developed anger toward the ministry. Because of the crisis of meaning that I was going through, I slowly went into maintenance mode. I also adapted some typical pastoral qualities, since I could not perform as a revivalist or as a church entrepreneur—the 24-hour smiler, the reconciler, the untiring visitor, the amusing Sunday orator, and the gentle voice in heated board meetings. I performed this way mostly with good intentions.

But to be successful in this function, I had to mask my inner crisis, and suppress all appearances of melancholy, complaint, or unpolished tone. After all, I was the spiritual leader and the model of anger management. I also thought that maybe this was a better path to attain authenticity. Ironically, I got angrier, because I had to subdue anger. It was a perfect environment to incubate a Shadow.

Another contributing factor to this dilemma was my lack of skill to navigate the middle way of work ethic—or everything under the sun. But career-wise, I went from assertive leadership to pathetic inclusivism; from authority over others to the suppression of oneself. Anger convinced me that this unhealthy transition is both a case of circumstantial trap and vocation incompatibility. It was enough for me to cultivate resentment with both my workplace and my faith journey.

Second, I nurtured anger toward the church. And every time I read the gospel, I got angrier. Mainly because I barely saw a resemblance between the early believers and us—the so-called modern-day church. Somehow, in the course of our advancement, we lost the passion and innocence of our teenage years: where religious virtue was not a ground for superiority, but a contribution to the larger vision of human awakening; where witnessing was not a denominational interest, but a manifestation of a life-altering encounter with the risen Christ.

Instead, we now look at our skyscrapers and boast of our influences, institutions, and equities. We quote the Scriptures to validate our creeds. We create systems that do more deferments than healing. We defend the status quo in the name of heaven. We are sounding more corporate than communal, more marketable than missional. We act as if we are owners of both the Scriptures and Jesus Christ. The last time I checked, the Son of Man was still bigger than our cathedrals, and the church was still beyond the confines of our political affiliations and Christian antiquities.

This may be how we got worse: when we overemphasized our divine sonship, our royal priesthood, and our chosen status. It was when our truth-claims became walls and the Great Commission turned messianic. As a result, we detached ourselves from the human community—its sweat, starvation, stench, and nightly screams.

After a while, I started seeing myself in the midst of this dark diatribe. My house was inside a huge but defective glass basilica. I was angry with the church but I was angrier with the reflection I see in its flawed walls—myself. I was irritated with my own imperfections, hardheadedness, and delinquency. It seemed that I cannot stand going down with people that carry the same paralysis as mine. Or probably being with them constantly reminded me of my own inability to change.

Am I a reflection of the filthy bride?
Am I the leprous-stricken body of Christ?
Am I the desecrated temple?
Am I the church that I am angry with?

Then there was my anger toward God. Why hide, and then demand faith? Why sit on your hands and watch us slaughter each other? Why put perimeters around space-time and leave us desperately wondering the beyond? Why give us the gift of fascination with the curses of chronology, gravity, and death?

These were questions I heard myself asking inside my prayer room. I would have been branded as a heretic if anyone heard it. So I only threw these fatal inquiries to God. It was similar to imprecatory and angry prayers that were sung by the Psalmist. So I felt justified for its tone of cynicism.

Sometimes, it was purely academic. Primarily, however, my questions were conceived by anguish and confusion. Later on, it was my discontent that turned this same anger into a destructive fuel. From a healthy practice of releasing toxic thoughts, it turned into uncontrollable skepticism and eventually mutating into a fire-breathing dragon.

Its beastly figure outshined the other shadows that prowled outside. It howled while it sharpened the tip of some long fiery darts. It appeared that he was suffering from a chronic wound at his left chest. This made the howling creepier and the night viler.

ALIENISM

Some have large oval eyes attached in an enormous head. They are the usual abduction suspects and are blamed for lost cows and strange crop circles. There are those who are objects of sick male fantasy—the angelic and luminous fairy-like blondes called Nordics. Then there are the insectoids and cyborgs–one stinky and the other techy. And lastly, those super gross amoebic blobs that see earthlings as an intergalactic all-you-can-eat buffet. These are some of the fictional aliens I remember watching out of the hundreds created by Hollywood.

But there is nothing more haunting than the prawns. They are the extraterrestrial creatures made by Neil Blomkamp in the film *District 9*. Unlike classical Star Trek plots, in this movie, the alien refugees are the victims of xenophobia and segregation. And the themes that held me most were homelessness, homesickness, and home invasion—space guests trapped in ghettos, ill longing for home, inability to assimilate, and the inhumane alienation engineered by the host—us!

I was an alien. As far as I can recall, I was always the most withdrawn, secretive, and oddly eremite kid in the house—whether it was in my family, church, or school. It was nobody's fault, not even mine. But it was in isolation that I find a momentary haven from threats of rejection, my shyness-causing pimples, intimidating cute girls, and *aswang* (Filipino vampires) by my bedroom window. So I created an alien of myself—the weirdo, the offbeat, and the suspicious at times. Or to put it in another way, I was the haunted house on the hill that townspeople avoided but loved to talk about.

When I entered the ministry, it was no surprise that I was immediately drawn to the esoteric life. But it was pastoral duties that taught me to be a social being. So from the woods I relocated to a bible-belt village where I learned to live the so called "higher calling"—extrovertism. It was enough to make me normal, to a certain extent. But while the house exhibited an appearance of openness, there were still traces of alienism inside. It was actually a strong asset in the Mystic room. But it seems that all its potentialities were not able to surpass its weaknesses.

I was an alien. And my alienism worsened when I left my homeland and migrated to a society whose dominant ideals are founded in individualism, self-reliance and privacy. Furthermore, this estrangement got tangled up with other complicated baggage I carried: my postcolonial concerns; my struggle with homesickness; and a troubling ambiguity with my own cultural identity.

I came from a people who struggle to reclaim their collective identity that was lost during years of colonization. Though the invader's hordes, tanks, and battleships left a long time ago, the painful memory of subjugation still lingers in the mind of our elders. Though our children can now lift a free flag and sing a national anthem in their schools, the poisons of slavery have already damaged the faith and confidence of those who are meant to prepare their way. We were a wretched protean house, raped, exploited, and altered by various intruders. We were aliens in our own homeland. And to some extent we still are in the grand machinery of expansionism.

I am a Filipino. What in *Pasig* does that even mean? Does it even matter if answers lie in the pre-magellanic time? Or is the cure found in the embrace of our evolving plurality?

And so like most immigrants, I brought these uncertainties and feelings of inferiority in diaspora life. Many times, withdrawal is the only place of safety. I was grateful the Mystic room was there with me. It became my sanctuary, my home. Sometimes, however, when I stayed in this room too long, I noticed a small dark fog forming at the right side of the sacrificial altar. I simply ignored it at first. But as the fog gently spread across the room, I got habituated to the relief and security its dimness gave. There I could not see my face, my failure, my location. There I could be bare, angry, and alone. The embrace of darkness was unconditional, I thought. The fleeting solace it brought felt so addictive and enthralling.

But dark clouds don't give free gifts, I later learned. It soon lured me into its depths where my depression was further soaked in grave isolation. There, daily devotions sounded more like self-pity sessions. Tongues turned into groaning. Prayers were mostly repentance because I was too broken to offer intercession for others.

I decided to take action. But when I entered the Mystic room that day, the dark cloud was not there anymore. I searched and found it in the basement, and it transformed into something else. It turned into one of them—a devious Shadow. I was startled while enticed with its stillness at the same time.

"No one will understand; no one cares; no one but the Shadow," I thought as I approached its luring shade.

Like a black hole, it quietly sucked energy and light out of me, reflecting nothing back. Darkness prevailed, time distorted, gravity warped as I neared my nervous breakdown.

ANXIETY

From the filthy environment that the other Shadows created, there ascended a hideous beast. It emanated anguish, panic, and dread. It was a Shadow called Anxiety.

I read about it, counseled its victims, and wondered at times how it rose to prominence in the psychiatric ward and how massive the damage it created in countless lives. I used to mock its old school tactics during spiritual warfare gatherings. I cursed its name on many occasions as I declared salvation to its prisoners.

Now the story had been entirely overturned. As I fell helpless on its feet, I watched its force ruthlessly invade my dwelling. An awful stench crawled slowly from its den filling each part of the house with toxicity and paralysis. Meaninglessness darkened each room. Paranoia sealed all entrances. The sound of glory was silenced. Portraits were veiled. Furniture corroded. Pillars impaired.

I called some close friends. But it was already too late. The poison was too thick for any antidote. The damages done were too severe for repair. As I looked in the eye of the inevitable, I was thrown back to a corner where I accidentally found my lost broken hammer.

I held it tight and whispered to myself, "This is no longer a home, but a lair of demons," as I prepared for the final battle.

four

I Am Homeless

THE STENCH of homelessness is hard to forget. It is the scent of despair and deprivation. Some stay under flyovers. Children that sleep in staircases of rail transits. Beggars sit in the marketplace. Families scrape rubbish in a smoky landfill. Millions of squatters compress beside city railways. And probably the worst I saw: slum dwellers residing inside local cemeteries. Homeowners called them the "living dead."

This is not something I watched on the 11 o'clock world news. I came from the Philippines. I was a firsthand witness. I entered their illegal shanties and felt the heavy chain of poverty. I extended my hands to some of them and offered meals, clothing, and community. I shared the good news of redemption. But more than the things I can remember doing, I will not forget something I did not see—I really did not believe their fate would change. After all, it never occurred to me that a day would come that I would be one of them.

I am homeless.

And thoughts of leveling the place began when the plague seemed irremediable.

BREAKDOWN

It was mostly pitch black on the days that followed. I could not remember where precisely in the house I began pummeling. It was hard to tell because of the suffocating darkness. But I believe I started where I fixed the sledgehammer—in the Servant room. That room was so plagued with the pathology of perfectionism. I hammered both my inventory of failures and the scale I used to assess my performance. I tore apart my clergy apparels—from robes to homilies, from crucifixes to shawls. I smashed the plaques against the portable podium and pulled the carpeting apart. I followed this destructive pattern as I roamed from one room to another.

With a crowbar, pry bar, jackhammer, nail puller and every demolition tool I could muster, I pulverized bricks, pulled wires, smashed walls, and sliced water pipes. I broke most of these tools before I finished breaking the house. I was not really following any demolition protocol—no permit, no neighborhood notification, no protection suit, and no logical procedure. There was only a lot of kicking and screaming. Again everything was happening inside. When I started ripping the exterior apart, neighbors started asking and I started inventing stories. "This is an HGTV-inspired makeover," was the easiest leave-me-alone excuse.

In spite of this chaos however, I was able to avoid anticipated complaints. I rented a dumpster and threw all asbestos, chemicals, and other contaminants in their proper disposal. I put a barrier around the perimeter so the debris would be contained. I could not, however, remedy the eyesore issue. I was aware that I left the site with unpleasant scenery—huge columns sticking out, dangling walls, and half of the roof hanging for its dear life. Its overall appearance created a disturbing image at night.

About the roof's other half, it caved in on me when my anxiety was critically high. That incident ended the demolition and strangely it started a healing process inside. Early the next morning when other pastors stood behind pulpits, I laid down in a stretcher to be brought to a behavioral hospital.

In the lobby, they sat me in an armchair where I was told to wait. In front of me was a dispensary where patients lined up for their medication. After half hour of almost motionless sitting, someone asked my name. I tried to ignore him but he was oddly insistent. I think he had a personality disorder. Though annoying, he was the first one who made me feel welcome in the house of bonkers.

It was either the lighting or the medication I was taking, but it was usually bleak in that infirmary. Or maybe it was just me and the emotional flu I was suffering from. But needless to say, I felt hopeless, confused, degraded. I looked back and I saw the run-down wreckage of my failure. I stared at a mirror and saw nakedness and shame. I tried to envision the future and I saw nothing. Nothing.

But on the third day, while we gathered for a group meeting in a secured room, a small light flickered. As the room was filled with tales of breakdown and resignation, I saw the unfolding of pure openness. The radiance of childlikeness touched my decaying soul as each of us confessed our feeling of powerlessness before depression. My mask of spirituality melted as I surrendered to the benediction of my own bitter narrative. For the first time in many years, I felt genuinely real.

And then I experienced something else, something strange. I started to realize that I was numbered among them—the ill, the disabled, the confused, the weak. For years, I was the healer. There I was numbered with the sick. The funny thing is it felt okay. I played a stupid board game with a confused lady and a recovering drug dependent. I ate meals together with mental patients, separated from the table of sophisticated-looking nurses and physicians. Unexpectedly, I felt peaceful to be identified with those who were diagnosed as chemically-deficient people. Right there, I saw that same distant gleaming light again.

After I got discharged, it suddenly hit me that I had no place to go. I lost both my home and reputation.

I walked passed my broken house, barely looking at it. I picked up what was left of the broken hammer and I just started to walk away. I continued walking until the road ended the next morning. Behind the sign that says "dead end," there was a small pathway hidden among the thick vines of a banyan tree. I sat under its comforting shade, closed my eyes, and asked myself what time it was.

Right before I drifted into sleep, I heard a voice saying, "Well, it depends."

"Who said that?" I asked startled.

"Mi," the voice replied.

"Who are you?'

"I already told you. My real name is Miriam. But my friends call me Mi," said an old woman in a colorful salwar and faded jeans.

She emerged from the other side of the trunk chewing on what seems to be dry roots of the banyan. After spitting a masticated handful, she pointed out that it's good for the teeth and a cure for infertility. She burst into a big laugh before offering me some. I think I communicated my disgust really well.

"So, you want to know what time it is?"

"It doesn't matter. Thanks anyway," I replied as I attempt to end the conversation. I failed.

> On the West Coast, they are still in bed. On the other side of the globe, they are about to have supper. Most will not be successful though. If you are in a train that can travel at 1,000 miles per hour, your time will be behind by a few billionths of a second to someone on the ground looking at the train. If your train can travel the speed of light, then the difference could be years. Are you on the train or not? They call this theory time dilation. Maybe Solomon was right when he said that there is time for everything. Its ten after six, by the way.

"Five days with the loonies were enough," I muttered to myself as I tried to walk away.

"Are you lost? Are you looking for a place to stay?

Though I was not planning on admitting it, I said yes.

"Well, we all feel that way sometimes. But they say that getting lost is part of the journey home," she stressed.

"There is an abandoned train carriage on the top of a hill just ahead. It's not much but maybe it can be a home for a few days. Just don't try to repair and run it. I think it needed to sit there for a while."

She was munching a few more roots as I was leaving. I'm not sure if she heard me say thanks.

"Just follow the tracks and you'll find it," she yelled.

And I did. When I first saw the shack, I instantly felt a strange connection with it. It was worse than I imagined, but I could not think of a more suitable place to stay. It doesn't seem to mind that some of its wheels were missing because its whole body was elevated from the ground by some six huge wooden planks under it.

It was a portrayal of rest.

I cleaned up one corner, tweaked a few small bars and joined a few seats to create a bed and partitions. I found a broken shelf and used it to hold the stuff I got from the landfill.

Days have passed and I am still here in this remote place, recuperating, hibernating, and holding on. I don't know what's going to happen next.

Wait, they are inside—the Shadows. I can hear them. They've broken through.

Words…these could be my last. I will write again, if I survive this dark night.

BURNING BUSH

These are my first words in ink after a week of pure awe. I am not dead, apparently. But what transpired since the evening of my last journal entry until today is beyond life-death stories. Allow me to take you back to the shack on that dreadful moment when the fangs of my own Shadows were literally on my throat.

I was still holding my pen when I felt their presence encircling me. I don't need to open my eyes to attest who they were. Or maybe I was just too scared to look. But while my eyes were shut, I saw that small light again flashed in a mental vision. It was serene, ethereal, a glimpse of the eternal. But it seemed so distant. I tried to approach it, but I was reminded of my imminent death. So at that split second when I sensed the Shadows' move to strike, I opened my eyes and gazed at the hollow face of the Absurd coming toward me. And there before the gates of hades, the unimaginable happened.

From where I was seated, my soul transcended to a place where I became an observer of space-time continuum, which at that moment seemed to be suspended. Below, I could view myself and the Shadows motionless on a bafflingly frozen terrain. I noticed that I was ascending due to a gentle gravitational pull from deep space. As I floated upward, everything visible gradually faded until I reached the realm of pure nothingness.

There were no emotions, no images, no sounds, and no dimensions.

Though there was no more reference point, I could tell that I was traveling faster, until I progressed beyond the speed of light. I yielded to this intelligent flow as it carried me to the vast unknown. After awhile, I realized that I was moving toward that small mystifying light I had seen in my earlier visions. Suddenly, I was in front of its holy presence.

It was the Tree of Life.

It was covered with flames that do not burn. The light it radiated was *understanding* and the fruit it bore was *healing*.

When I attempted to get nearer, I heard a voice saying, "Take off your garments, for this is holy ground."

I felt both shame and serenity as I obeyed and faced my own nakedness. But the radiance that emanated from the Tree of Life surrounded me with unconditional acceptance. The voice then asked about the sledgehammer in my hand. It was not a question that seeks facts and reason, because the one who spoke already knew. It sounded like Grace awaiting my return.

Before I could utter a word, an image of the wreckage I left appeared before me like a holographic flashback.

After a painful silence I said, "I lost it all. The house . . . it's all gone."

"It is time to let go," the voice replied.

I opened my calloused palm to release the sledgehammer I was holding for so long. It made its last pounding sound as it hit the surface of that celestial place. The dirt welcomed the trodden tool as how earth would receive lifeless bodies. As I was watching this burial, it slowly resurfaced from the soil that engulfed it, but it went through a significant change. It turned into a carpenter's hammer. From an instrument of demolition, it transformed into a symbol of restoration; from a deconstructive design to a creative function; the sledgehammer was now a tool for building. I picked it up while being told to start foreseeing anew.

"Who are you?" I asked.

The voice replied, "I AM."

Suddenly, my eyes were opened. Though I could gaze its fullness earlier, I started to see another dimension that was beyond forms I could perceive and notions I could absorb. The branches were extended across intercosmic space where they nurtured the spawns of infinite expansion. Its roots were spread out deep beneath the veil of planck time, where the laws of physics are restricted to explore. Its torso was a reflection of omnipotence and glorious beauty, where countless biospheres are still being created and where all civilizations are given birth. Its entirety is covered with radiance like that of a thousand supernova.

As I stared at it in fearful wonder, I fell at its feet as though dead.

BAMBOO TREE

When I woke up, I realized that I was carried back to the suspended space-time I left—same moment, same posture, same stench, and same hell. One thing was different though; I could still see the image of the Tree of Life across from where I was seated. The light that emanated from the celestial vision seemed to transfuse a passage through the darkness that impeded and the Shadows that surrounded me. I was then reminded that my clock was about to resume at any moment. And in a flash it did.

But for some reason, my expanding awareness transcended beyond the looming danger and the velocity of quantified time. I was aware of the swiftly approaching Shadows raving to devour me, but I was no longer afraid.

I stretched my right hand like I always did during pastoral benediction and whispered, I AM.

If this was a sci-fi story, the Shadows would shriek in terror as their eerie body consumed into ashes and their savage soul returned to hell.

Disappointingly, that was not what happened. There were no explosions, no music crescendo, no falling rubble, and no heroic pose at the backdraft of a burning building. Instead there was only a pleasant surrender aided by a higher insight of the Whole, the Connection, the Eternal, and the Home that shelters all.

There was no more resistance because, even before the crisis, there was really no disconnect, no otherness, no adversary, and thus no war. The Shadows were not alien entities. They were members of the Whole, sections of the house, parts of what I refer to as "I." So, there was no assault, no collision, and no casualty. Rather, it was a return, a healing hour, an awakened acceptance of what *Is*.

Though this was happening right in front of me, it appeared only as a background to a higher event that was simultaneously transpiring—the vision of the tree was fading in a peculiar way. The emanation of light was still evident, but it was not from the same Tree of Life anymore. The vision left, but its glory rested upon my young bamboo tree. It was then I realized that the physical features of the trees were similar, although I did not understand what this meant.

Maybe during the earlier trance, my subconscious used a familiar form so I could conceive the formless. Or maybe the temporal was significantly linked to the infinite. Or perhaps, in spite of their considerable distinction, the trees were, in actuality, the same in essence and purpose.

As mentioned earlier, a beautiful bamboo plant sprouted in the middle of the shack. The small crack on the metal roof allows the sun to give it morning greetings while I bring rainwater for its weekly drink. There is one culm in the middle and three rapidly growing shoots on each side. Its rhizomes are medicinal and its leaves are edible. Unlike most varieties of bamboos, this kind does not grow immensely. So its moderate height makes it an ideal indoor plant.

It was a faithful companion, especially when one is literally in the dump. The roots were deeply entrenched, but not dispersed all over. The branches were fanned out with a seemingly altruistic generosity. Its stability was impressed in its innate flexibility and stillness. Like a magical portal, it bridged earth and heaven and, while I was isolated, it connected me to life in the outside world. So prior to any of these magical events, the bamboo tree was already lovely, and to be covered with cosmic aura was even more glorious. But that was not even the amazing part.

As I beheld this apparition, all appearances of numinosity faded from the tree and its surroundings. That was the last time I had a spiritual vision. But instead of the gloominess returning, the dead space I was living in gradually brightened. I thought it was just some residue of the heavenly vision. It wasn't. Traces of the supernatural were gone.

The features of the room stayed the same. But like recovering from a long half-conscious state, I felt a strange but elated awakening of my senses. I could see more clearly. Before, all I saw in that dump was rust covering everything metal. I really did not pay any attention to the old glass windows that were held by stained duct tape; the tiny scrapings from the ceiling falling increasingly; my small soiled kitchenware that I placed in a broken bookshelf.

I also noticed that I could breathe with ease and felt a sense of pleasure as air passed my nostrils, even with the dampness. The noise of crickets and the singing of early sparrows, I heard them again. But that morning, it sounded almost melodic. The calmness that that isolated terrain offered became profoundly evident.

The ordinary, the familiar, and the routine—I could not dismiss them anymore or label them as trivial. They were part of the Whole. So when I experienced them, I encountered the splendid and mysterious universe in its entirety. Everything was connected. When I looked at the clouds above me, was I not also looking at the grandeur of the Orion nebula? When I touched the dirt underneath, was I not also touching the highest bedrock of Mt. Everest? In a single breath, am I not also participating in eternity? When I speak, am I not reverberating the sound of a thousand dialects?

Or when I am at peace, am I not manifesting that spiritual energy in my present surrounding?

And when I give a cup of water to the least of these, am I not quenching the thirst of Christ?

Again, the bamboo tree caught my attention. As I gazed at it, it felt like I was also beholding the same majesty that the celestial Tree radiates—a silent teacher, a sacred emblem, and a source of life. It saved me more than I served it.

I soaked the ground, dug around the roots, and gently lift it up from the soil. I placed it in a plant bag I'd been making with the materials I salvaged from the dump. I put the hammer in my tool belt, the pen and journal in my pocket. Then for the first time after many weeks of staying indoors, I stepped out.

It was time to go home.

I immediately felt the cold touch of the morning drizzle slowly drenching my shirt. I closed my eyes and turned my face toward heaven. Each drop of rain I caught was like cleansing suds that washed and refreshed my grimy and worn-out body.

Once more, I touched the leaves of the plant I was carrying on my back.

five

I Am

I AM Bolt. I am Baby Brent. I am Buzz Lightyear. These are lines of three animated characters from three different films, with one common overrated plot—*who am I?* Their stories started with heroism and certainty, only to be interrupted by a mid-plot crisis of identity. Bolt was a Hollywood-made super dog. Baby Brent was Swallow Fall's infant commercial model. And Buzz was a legendary space ranger from the Intergalactic Alliance.

Sadly, none of them were true.

Then, at a critical moment when breakdown was pulling them apart, they rediscovered their unconditional I-am-ness and felt wholeness for the first time.

Their stories mirror the individual and collective experience of many who go through the pain of existential crisis, and rose from it a changed conscious being—calm, compassionate, content, connected. Their dream world would try to drag them back, but the initial taste of awakening is worth far more than many imaginary castles. They are home.

I know that the lure of homelessness will come back strong. But I was not expecting that it would be that soon. Because just a few steps after I stepped out of the broken carriage, I felt a strange pull from inside me to go back to the dark cave of depression. The Shadows are always stronger when hidden and they will do anything to keep me from leaving the shack. So right there, while I sensed in my belly a threatening relapse, and while looking at the road that pointed back home, I uttered the *I Am* affirmations. I cannot remember the exact words I used, but I do remember the heart of that rather long discourse.

I opened my mouth and said, *I am*.

CONSCIOUSNESS, I AM

I am consciousness. Thus I am a witness. Thus I am soul. I transcend my identity—my thoughts, my feelings, my body. While participant in the valley of events and experiences, I also stand on a hill and see the wider landscape of existence. I am above circumstances, chaos, and continuance. I am an observer of the ever-present Grace that reminds me of my place in the infinite Whole. Thus I am humbled by the widening perception, inspired by the expanding cosmos.

I am aware of my awareness. I am aware that my awareness is finite. But it is this same awareness that makes me complete at any given moment: at peace with what *is*; accepting of what is not; intentional with choices; and yielded to evolving possibilities.

I am more than a determinant and a participant. I am a witness. I was once a believer of the value of control, until my hand broke due to over-clenching. In brokenness, I realized that I am simply a witness. I witness the magnificent unraveling of life everywhere. I witness process as it births change. I witness purity in the eyes of children. I witness wisdom as I listen to the raspy voice of an elderly person. I savor the richness of cultures in entrees and victuals. I feel the pulse of love within and around me. I breathe the unseen spiritual energy that sustains us all. I witness myself witnessing the splendor of the present moment.

I breathe. I am aware of my being. I am an inhabiting presence in this time and space. I am the self, the essence, the *I* who observes my beingness. Life after death is not more fascinating than life right now. I am alive and my aliveness radiates all beings and existences to which I am luminously connected.

COMPLETE, I AM

I am here. I am whole. I am beautiful. I am complete even now. The actual here and now is always Whole. Thus, there is unconditional contentment in the reality of my current state.

Here I am, in raw tenderness, present now. I enjoy this moment, the only time there is. I live on earth, the only planet I call home. There may be parallel universes beyond this cosmological horizon. I welcome this possibility without doubting the reality I know.

Here-*ness* is not geocentric, messianic, nor egocentric.

I am here, meaning I ascertain my presence with reverence, humility, and appreciation. I am here complete, delighting in what *Is*. And it is only in this here-*ness* that I am able to give myself to others.

I am beautiful. I am a work of art. Remove all the trimmings and labels and my essence will remain. Because, essentially, I am an emanation of goodness and beingness—the image of God.

In nakedness, I see austerity.

In silence, I hear poetry.

In imperfection, I radiate that constant Grace abundantly infilling.

There is nothing I could do to tarnish the divinity that dwells within now. There is no soul disconnected to the wonderful Whole, which I am a small part of. Our existential bond accentuates the encompassing glory that brightens us all.

I am complete. This knowledge is not a justification for indolence and irresponsibility. In the recognition of completion, one is grateful with unmerited gifts. Skills and resources are used to create, cultivate, and discover. The complete is developed to advance knowledge, create new paths, and fulfill visions. My completeness is meant to evolve, expand, and enhance.

But my journey is not anymore driven by heroism. I don't need a grand mission to experience meaning and worth. Authenticity is not an obsession any longer, or the intention of attaining it a necessity to establish an identity. What I've been through, where I am now, who I am becoming is enough to experience wholeness, because reality, by its very essence, is already Whole.

Feelings of incompleteness arise from judgment and the belief of disconnection. We judge others so we can hide our own inadequacy. We harbor insecurity because we feel deprived of things, qualities, and people we think we should have.

I am complete not because I claim authenticity and am in need of nothing. I am complete in spite of my inauthenticity, deficiency, and a yearning for God's mercy. I am complete because I am connected to the unconditional Whole. I am complete because I am a recipient of a full life bestowed by our heavenly Source, Sustainer, and Father.

COMPASSION, I AM

I am an emanation of Love, a small ray of the timeless stellar, a manifestation of salvific intent. I am a drop of that satiating fountain, a breath of the life-giving Pneuma, a piece of the unconditional earth, a single pulse of the sacred heart of Christ. I am created in the image of God. Thus I am compassionate. When I smile, I sow joy. When I sing, I release healing. When I write, I give voice to the unheeded. I am a passageway, an echo, a reflection of the greatest force in creation: Love.

I know my spiritual deformities. So I am not inferring stale piousness and I am too lazy to claim the immaculate. The capacity for compassion is a gift imparted in our primordial nature. It is basic goodness. It is God-bestowed. Yet in countless epochs and cultures, it got corrupted, commercialized, consumed in steeples, streets, and stock markets.

I realized that in caskets, cardboards, and Calvary, we recover it, if we look closer, or if we get lost enough. During this difficult season, we get wasted—enough to see things differently. We realized that there is a difference between a service-oriented career and acts of broken compassion. I, for one, was a public servant in a sacred robe. I wore the cross, an emblem of empathy. I carried anointing oil, the balm of Gilead.

And then the dramatic overturn. I became one of them—a vagrant in the land of wretchedness. For a while compassion died. Then there was a painful rebirth. But compassion, it seems, is not the same anymore . . . it got broken.

There is a strange aching inside as I began to feel for the "crazies" I am now identified with. There is genuine empathy for the emotionally disabled and deviant. There is an agonizing cry for the fatalities of an alienated world. But strangely, there is also this humbling helplessness to rescue any of them. Unlike before when I wore an armor of invincibility, now I feel so useless.

Brokenness impaired both my pride and fearlessness. I know that I will soon regain the emotional muscles I lost. But for now, compassion, it seems, is transforming slowly in a strange but tender way. My trumpets are all beaten down and the court mallets I used to hold were lost in the demolition. I gave up the robes and the camera is off.

Maybe love is naked so it can be trusted. Love is a wounded healer so it can be humble. Like a mother in birth pain, it goes through suffering while it delivers heaven.

I am capable of forgiveness because I was granted an immense pardon when I least deserved it. I am free of yearnings for recognition to feel significant and I do not condemn those who need it. I need no grand mission to harness the energy of compassion. Compassion is unconditional regardless of magnitude or meagerness. I am spacious enough to embrace the world; small enough to admire a worm.

I am a well-digger, a bridge-maker and a contented homemaker.

I am capable of anger without being its prisoner. I am good to myself. I forgive my flaws and celebrate my feats.

I am part of all, and connected to all. I am conceived in the eternal womb of Love and now interwoven in this vast ocean of compassion we call Spirit.

CONNECTED, I AM

I am a piece of the Cosmos. My single essence is inherently linked to the Whole. Meaning radiates in this pervading reality: One Verse. I receive life. I give life. I am a passageway. I am a connection, a bridge between the finished and the not yet, history and potentiality, yesterday and tomorrow. Thus, I will fulfill my purpose simply by being in the now—a present participant in the eternal continuum.

Witnessing this interconnection, there is a lesser need to assert, achieve, and acquire. There is trust in the nature of holons and the grace of synchronicity.

I do not need to judge others to promote my uniqueness. Not just because I now see elements of genius and sacredness in all things, but also because our every individual *essentia* are sustained by this all-pervading mystical circuitry.

Each consciousness, subatomic particles, organisms, civilizations, memes, aesthetics, spiritualities, ecosystems, biospheres, intercosmic symmetries are all part of this glorious reality we refer to as "Everything."

I used to only see reality in classifications, quadrants, hierarchies, colors, tribes, labels: there is devotion when villains are labeled; there is order when rulebooks are followed; there is sanctification when monasticism is practiced. Though categorization tutored me basic judgments, I am now beyond binaries, borders, and boxes. I am witnessing the beautiful interweaving of totality. I believe that this is how we compose music, discover depths, promote planetary harmony, alleviate hunger, and see a multidimensional universe.

When I live in connection, I am healed of harmful isolation. When I sensed connectedness, the awareness ripples in my environment. When I appreciate the Immanent, I also experience the Transcendent. When I see the face of Christ, I also see the face of the Father. I am complete because I am connected. I am connected because I feel complete. My connection completes the Whole. Others' connections marvelously complete me.

CALM, I AM

On this sphere called earth, I stand. My feet are steadily entrenched in the ground where all life is formed. There is nothing in it that I possess. Yet there is nothing that separates me from its care.

The Shadows are still near me: some prowl in silence while others show signs of change. But I am not afraid of fear anymore. I feel its early grip as it tries to reawaken Anxiety. Uneasiness creeps in as I anticipate the worst. Amazingly, however, I found myself unmoved, calm. It is not the absence of fear, but a sense of confidence to observe it come and go.

I am calm. In steadiness of heart, I am.

On this journey called life, I dance. I hear the music. I sense the flow. It is within and around me, beneath and upon me. I yield to the ever-graceful stream of transformation. I float in the vast field of potentiality. I drift in the flux of paradox. I trust the fluidity of existence. Thus I am calm.

I was once a guardian of parameters and establishments. Now I am part of the flow that is constantly unfolding; a dance in which all of nature participates.

It is a dance that is accompanied by a beautiful melody, inviting all to go with the leading of the Spirit.

It is therapeutic.

It is engaging.

It is calming.

At this time I call *now* I sat. I feel that some of the arrows I released yesterday are now directly above my head. And the worries of tomorrow are overspilling to my concerns today. I am seated, watching the pull of each time pole. The past reminded me of my loss. The future threatened me with uncertainties. Both are compelled to remove me from where *I am*. I realized then that the very ability to observe this struggle is the source of the inner calmness I am presently experiencing.

Yes, I am calm.

six

I Am Home Always Already

AFTERWARD, I stopped and allowed silence to pervade...

I finally released words . . . words that I have to say. There was nothing in my past that prepared the Shadows for this response. We usually met in the air for spiritual combat. But at that moment, there was only surrender, strength in enlightened surrender. It was a force they could not understand. It was a confession they could not contain. It was an acceptance they could not defy.

After saying these words, an unseen shackle was broken.

I slowly trod down the trail of the hill that led me to the road back home. The rain has stopped, leaving a pleasant scent and a muddy breakdown lane. The sun is out, drying the moisture the rain just created. The Shadows are more visible in the light. To say the least, they did not enjoy the journey with the fine sun glinting at them.

After a few miles of hike, I saw Miriam again. She was in the middle of a field together with some young people. It appeared like they were building a boat. With dirt still on her hands, she stretched them toward me and gave me a benediction—in pure silence and with a smile that seems to say, "I know." It was sufficient to inspire me for a nonstop all-night trip treading the byways and hitching cars.

Later that night, I remembered my encounter with Miriam. I was too far to comprehend their conversation, but I was close enough to hear the young people calling her "Iam."

"Maybe another nickname," I said to myself.

And then it hit me!

Was it a coincidence that my source of deliverance is reflected in her name? Is she some sort of a sage or an oracle? I don't know. But the connection of all these recent events in my life was too ingenious to be taken lightly.

Early the next morning, I arrived home, or what was left of it. The parameter was still secured and the debris was all contained. For a moment, I allowed an intense feeling of grief to emerge and then fade. After finding a temporary space for the bamboo plant, I made a quick inventory of items in the wreckage that remained intact and those that are still reusable.

Engaged in digging, I did not notice that a few of my neighbors were gathered on what used to be a front porch, watching me like I was staging a home makeover episode. Encouraging words were said. Help was offered, suggestions were expressed and expectations were laid.

"What kind of neoeclectic design are you going to apply to your new house?" one asked teasingly.

It was then that I realized that a few unorthodox homeowners had already moved in the neighborhood.

"It seems that the eco-friendly, the unconventional, and the almost comical are now redefining architecture around here," I muttered to myself.

Right across from us is a house that depicts an illusion of being suspended in midair. The roof of a three-story pineapple is visible blocks away. I later called the owner Spongy. I noticed a house that is obviously engineered by a rock star . . . or woodpeckers. There was a minka in Victorian landscape; a spaceship house in '60s vintage; and a couple of 65-square-feet miniscule homes.

"After all, isn't it that renovation is the reason why you demolish your old house in the first place?" interrupted another.

Before I can respond, a young lady in a beautiful kanga attire handed me a card introducing herself as a general contractor for a company that specializes in remodeling.

"We know why people demolish houses. You are searching for a better home and we are here to make sure you'll get it," she explained convincingly.

"What are my options?" I replied.

She looked at the rubble I was filling up earlier and said, "Renovation and renewability: this is one of our axioms. Rebuild anew with layouts of postmodernity and renewable energy as your underlying concept. This is the home that you are looking for."

Nodding their heads gently, the people gathered seem to agree with the proposal. I stooped down to pick up a leaf that fell from the bamboo tree. It was soft, fresh, and calming as always. I put it in my pocket as I stood up. Then I began to speak.

> I was doubtful this day would ever come that I would be welcomed again. But you all made sure it would. With your help, a second chance is possible for me. You know that I have always been a

> restless seeker. With all sincerity and stupidity, I sought a home. This search led me from home-ownership to homesickness to homelessness; from living in a castle to squatting in cardboards, to lying nearly dead in a carriage-made casket.
>
> And then I realized something that is only learned in deepest pain: that I am home, always already. I have always been. I will always be. This land is home. This earth is home. This moment is home for us all. I will rebuild, but I am not sure if I will relocate or stay. I am all for change, but I am not sure if I really need a new blueprint. I left the shack yesterday. But I am not sure if I will start construction today. I came back with all these uncertainties. I came back hoping that I could find some answers in this wreckage below me. I'm just glad that even this state of reluctance is unconditionally sheltered under the all-pervading at-homeness we all share.

I got a response similar to a congregation on a Sunday morning with their glows, glares, and grogginess. Two people in suits listening from the back went away abruptly. Tree huggers crossed their arms. Some were looking through me as they tried to recognize the shadowy figures hiding behind my back. Enthusiasm turned cold, gradually expressing pity.

And then there were a few whose eyes glowed as if we came out from the same womb. They saw beyond religious modus and postmodern faddism. They were homeowners, but they exceeded the concrete walls of houses, for the whole cosmos was for them a vast place of love and possibility. These were the same people who helped me in the process of recovery.

That same day, I built a small shed where I stayed temporarily until I was strong enough to work. I found the old blueprint and played with possible alterations. Surprisingly, the large beams and slabs were still in good condition; some of the concretes and woods were still reusable; and the water and electricity was not yet cut off. I hung the hammer by the wall hoping that I could get some guidance or inspiration as I look at it daily.

In spite of the ambiguity and blank pages, I brought the hammer down one day, got a few more tools and started a sequence of restoration. I gathered the pieces of the broken rock, which stood before as the central figure of the former house. It was a symbol of certitude and stability. When I saw it that day in fragments and shreds, I felt both fear and brokenness.

I then ground it and mixed a portion of it in the concrete I used for the foundation. I stored the rest in the shed so I could use it later for the driveway and landscaping.

I set the bamboo tree at the center of the house where the rock used to be esteemed and adulated. I also framed the walls, attached the sheathings, and secured the trusses. The space is enclosed but still unfinished; insufficient yet habitable. I cannot proceed beyond that point. Not yet.

I mentioned earlier that I did not experience anymore spiritual vision since the Tree of Life epiphany. Well, not until today. Though I cannot describe it as similar to a cinematic vision, it was nonetheless parallel in energy and substance.

This morning, while attending to the bamboo tree, I sensed my awareness heightened and my spirit expanded. I did not stop what I was doing. Just like other days, I gave the tree a small amount of water and removed the dried leaves from its branches. It is now a few inches higher than when I first brought it in. In fact, I think I counted more nodes today than yesterday.

While amazed at the depth of my awareness with something so common, I started to sense the house in its entirety—its dimensions, paint, furniture, lighting, and incompleteness. It was a knowing of what Is; a witnessing of that which was always there. It was experiencing the ordinary and the routine with lesser judgment. It was that which I sought all my life, but I kept on missing because I was always looking beyond the normal.

It was the planet I missed admiring because I was waiting for a new heaven and new earth; the hungry bodies I did not feed because I was too busy saving souls; relationships I did not enjoy because I was too occupied with goals; the success I did not celebrate because it wasn't good enough; the places I left due to restlessness; the food I ate but did not savor because of guilt; the praises I refused because I felt undeserving; the day off I did not enjoy because I was thinking of work; the workday I dragged my robe up to the pulpit because I wished it was my day off; the spirituality I could not attain because I was waiting for the ecstatic; answers I did not find because I was using the benchmark of certainty; the man Jesus I seldom read because of a divine Christ I needed daily.

It was the present, the raw, the childlike, and the naked real—they were all there at that moment, as they have always been. I felt the aliveness that is entrenched in parts and portions of the house. Though the interior waterfall was destroyed, I could sense an unseen stream that filled the empty spaces. Though the rock of stability was broken, the bamboo tree radiated with strength and contentment. Though the Shadows stayed entangled in dark corners of the basement, they created channels where God's grace flowed and filled the house. Though there were walls I still cannot measure, rooms I cannot name, sections that remained open, I am home nonetheless.

And even when I go outside to explore, I am still home. Like turtles that carry their houses with them, at-homeness shelters me beyond fixed locations. Thus, not being home is not necessarily homelessness. Sometimes it just means I'm having an outdoor adventure. In fact, I now believe that there is no place in the universe where homelessness is found, because it is the very presence and awareness of the eternal I AM that makes any place a home.

And so, even if there are homes and communities I can never be part of, neighbors I cannot please, and homeowners' standards I can never meet, I am home always already.

Whether I grow old in a foreign land or go back to my homeland; whether I am tried in a defective courthouse or thieves make dens in my prayerhouse; though media houses are increasingly politicized, and houses of learning are downsized; though bars and coffee houses are now more welcoming than churches, food banks, and hospitals; though many science labs turned stale, and industrialization exploited our only home planet; though we continue to create fences instead of flyovers, competitions than potential collaboration . . . this neighborhood, this land, this society, this culture, this world *is* home. I am home always already.

And though in the past, world leaders led us to bomb each other's houses down; though scientists, sages, and civic servants abandoned the bridges between them; though we the whole human community could not yet see one home called earth, instead we see borders, regions, tribes, cultures, denominations, and skin colors; and though God seems silent with our demand for explanation, leaving us orphans in the infinity of mazes and hour glasses . . . we are home.

This faith, this soul, this ego, this body, this crowded city or this virgin forest, this nation-state, this civilization, this ecosystem, this epoch, this story, this vast cosmos, this is our home—with its birth pains, its riddles, its shadows.

From the convoluted shanties in Manila to suburban cities in Toronto; from the orphanages in South Africa to adult communities in Florida; from the forest of the Amazon to prison cells in Guantanamo; from boathouses to skyscrapers; from refugee camps to underground churches; from the White House to Imperial Palaces; from Buckingham Palace to all Palacio de Gobierno; from cottages of queens to retreat houses of presidents; from Malacanang to Groote Schuur; from the United Nations to the chapels of the Vatican; this is our home.

From earth to unknown goldilocks planets; from our solar system to other planet-hosting stars; from the depth of our consciousness to the depth of space; from this life to life eternal . . . this is our home.

And so, at times, I will feel homeless, homesick, or homebound with strange shadows in my basement, God is there to remind me of who I am, where I am, that I am home always already.

At-homeness is not meant to overlook the reality of evil. On the contrary, the experience of home is the integral inception of the personal and global transformation we all long for. It is the home that we tried running away from in hope that we could find a better world. But the world we seek for tomorrow is only conceivable through a spiritual and global homecoming we can actualize today.

This is my fourth journal entry and the second time I am writing in a shack. But this is a different shack, and only a few miles from my house. Yes, I am back squatting, but only for a day or two, or who knows. The one staying here is now asleep. He doesn't know yet that I'm here, though he is expecting my coming. He should, because he was the one who invited me and four others to come and visit him. The rest of the guests should be here by tomorrow morning, including Miriam.

I still don't know what to tell him. I know his questions, but I'm not ready to articulate answers. I can relate with the pain of homelessness, but I feel disconnected with his generation. I want to appear confident without giving a proud impression. What would I say?

As I reflected on these things, I stepped out of his shack—a broken observatory beside a hidden lake. The tall steel beams beneath us gave me a panoramic view of this secluded place. The calm water that vividly reflects the beauty of heaven inspired me to pen my thoughts.

But looking further, I could also see dark clouds forming on every direction. Unrest is building up with renewed force in lands of ancient symmetrical homes, generating both optimism and fear.

In the same way, the short hike coming here was both inspiring and burdening. I met travelers on the road: some hiking together, some wandering alone, all are searching for home. Written on each of their faces are something familiar—wonder, restlessness, discontent. All of them were lacking meaning, maps, and mentors. Most were zeekers and boomers, pans and x'ers. Though each generation crossed paths, most don't seem to find affinity with each other. They usually traveled with those coming from the same epoch.

Some travelers turned settlers. Each of their houses exhibited their own configurations, calibers, and conditions. Some are in the early phase of construction, while others are getting ready for demolition. Some built high walls and garrisons because expanding homes turned dominantly imperial. Some made a spectacle of the mudslinging between the house of progressives and the conservatives, unions and lawmakers, the prolife and the prochoice, the socialists and the capitalists, the monotheists and the pantheists; between the theocratic, the monarchical, and the republic; or between the pacifists, the activists, and the patriotic; the idealists the non-aligned, and the bulwark of institutions; while others complained that mud-making was prohibited in their homes.

I uttered a silent prayer, that a natural process of home building may gradually take place in all lives, homes, and nations—a process not designed by arrogance, attachments, or assertions. Rather, may it be the unfolding of an evolving life-force, where wisdom is incarnated in the architecture, and the needed energy is supplied by mutual compassion. And then I said,

> Lord, many ages have passed since you left your heavenly home, emptied yourself, and dwelled among us. Through your love, you restored broken homes, and by your power, you tore down empires and kingdoms. You taught us to love our neighbors, and preach good news throughout the world. You pointed us to a place where houses are not devoured by thieves nor corrosions; a kingdom not far away nor forthcoming.
>
> But a kingdom at hand. A home always already.
>
> And then the men in robes, those who claimed they lived in the house of Solomon, came and destroyed your temple, your body, your home. But after three days, you showed to us your words were true—the kingdom that is at hand is eternal. Your temple was restored, your body resurrected, your home was rebuilt into a glorified presence.
>
> And so may we, residents of one world—the homeless, the homebuilders, the homeowners—may we find at-homeness in the humbling experience of homelessness; may more bridges be built between homeowners; and may we have a collective awakening in this house that is always already our home where we share this fascinating and terrifying existence with the whole human community and the continuously all-constructing reality.

He's awake. I think I now know the first thing I want to say to him.

"Welcome home Peter Pan, welcome home."

seven

I, Others, and the Pan

I LOOKED at him straight in the eye. They were blank. There was very little trace of the Pan I watched flew when I was young. His sparkle was gone. His sword was rusted. His magic pouch was almost empty.

An architect of change, stricken with paralysis; a lead millennial for tomorrow's world, yet deeply troubled by the uncertain; a model builder among dreamers, but that night, he was numbered among the homeless.

"Simon. Call me Simon," he replied.

He closed his eyes and was awakened the next day by the clatter of pans hitting the kitchen door. It was the third time Miriam attempted to open that door quietly. She failed in all three but that last one was a siren. Her apology was interrupted by the arrival of other guests.

It was already Friday morning.

The greeting was short but heartbreaking. Even the callous face of a drifter named Neil was quickly smitten with grief. Raised from a clan of gun makers, he studied forensic science, developed his skill with firearms, and later became a bounty hunter. He came that day with his classic camouflage uniform tucked in a leather jacket as obnoxious as his opinions. I can tell that he already surveyed the place before showing up on the front door.

Paul on the other hand was not wearing his clerical robe and collar. For him it was more than his weekly pastoral visitation. He left his parish so he can devote a few days attending to Peter.

"The Teacher would have done the same," he said.

Then there was Era. Her hair pretty much says it all. It's long and braided at the end with a tie-dye headband in front. She wore a long skirt she brought from Geneva last year where she gave a presentation in an inter-religious dialogue. Though she's already in her 50's, traces of youth-energy were still visible on her neck and arms. Era is Peter's aunt, but she is better known to many as "the mentor."

As we gathered around Peter, a long silence prevailed in the room. Actually, no one dare say a word for a whole day. Axioms of sympathy would just sound so cold; psychotherapy seemed mockery; all forms of exhortations and catchphrases of religion would just fall short. Somehow words were forgotten, right there on that sacred moment to give way for the emanation of such piercing stillness—a pervading facilitator of harmony and restoration.

And like a subtle glasscutter, it slowly incised holes in our walled courage so some glimmer of vulnerability will illumine that dark metallic space. In the depth of silence, there emerged some faint sounds: a fizzled sob, a painful hum from wounded healers, a whispered prayer for a helpless comrade.

And without the aid of hollow theorems, spiritual knitting took place between friends and rivals—a premature healing that will just be apprehended again by differences.

After a while it seemed safe to break the silence but no one was brave enough to go first. Then a creepy screeching sound reverberated across the hall that leads underneath.

"I swear, that sounded like my mother-in-law on my wedding day," Miriam finely remarked.

Afterward, she took a loud sip of what I suspected as her infamous banyan tea from a mug that has a butt drawn on its bottom. I never found mother-in-law humor funny, but the mug brought the money home. When I was ready to burst, knowing that I would probably be given a liturgy-pill to be quiet, Pan erupted with a huge laugh. One by one, we joined into what seemed to be like a grand chorus of child-like hoopla.

While enjoying that light moment, I can see a figure coming out of the dark hall, across from where I and Miriam stood. On his left hand he was holding what seems to be like a long panga and on his right he was dragging a wounded prey. It was Neil and he was not laughing.

He threw the dying victim in the middle of the room like a prized plunder and with a gruesome Freddy-Krueger-tone he said, "Welcome to Neverland."

Era screamed her lungs out with an ear-piercing wail. I think she made her shock and bitter protest really really clear.

"You . . . don't . . . kill . . . a shadow! Not anymore!" she yelled.

Paul, with both disgust and cautiousness on his face, approached the dark form slowly. "Oh is that what it is? Nice cut!" he remarked.

And that was the start of a long theatrical polemics with characters as bad as a delayed presidential debate.

Era asserted, "Nice cut? Nice cut? Wait are we doing preschool chain crafts to grade our cutting skills? Please tell me so I can go back home and get my safety scissors! Nice cut . . . Are you even sure it's a shadow? What if it's an undiscovered organism or a dark nephilim or a . . ."

"Okay, that's enough!" Paul interrupted. "We don't want to hear any more mythical creatures from your interfaith lexicon!"

After a slight chuckle, Era answered back saying, "Well first of all, all faiths are interfaith, even your little conventional box. Second, I did not come here to watch the slaughter of everything you consider as 'others.' I came here for Peter. And I don't think a carnage show will be good therapy for him right now."

Neil, with his usual derisive talk laid down his counter argument,

> Well, well, well. If it isn't the prophet of kumbayah who promotes universal ideals on one hand and suppresses the postcolonial cause on the other; who would rather save an endangered salmon than a living fetus; the tree hugger who values the forest over her civilization, or her government, or her loved ones; who labels order and control as imperialistic, nihilistic, or even demonic.
>
> So tell me really, who has a more venomous blade: the bounty hunter or the closed aunt who wears a lot of pockets?

He then turned to Peter and said, "Hey Pete, be careful. You never know if your ruin will come from your own house."

"You bastard," Era scoffed.

Neil raised both hands in the air, gesturing concede while holding a smirk that said, "Gotcha!"

Era turned to her niece and asked, "Peter, how are you feeling?"

Sitting up from where he was resting, which seemed to be a broken lab table, he pointed to the slain and uttered with a grating voice, "that's my Shadow."

It was only then that we noticed something bizarre. We had heard stories of white shadows in the past, but none among us in that room had ever seen one, until that moment when the fetid grease it amassed from the basement gradually faded revealing its true ghostly surface.

It was mostly robe—priestly and primeval—that was formed like limbs, head, and hem. In some few angles, one could see it emanating what seemed to be ancient algorithms in fluctuating waves. Though faceless, it telepathically conveyed a terrifying sense of dread, which really crept our guts out. The expressions from each of our faces were the same: confusion, cowardice and concern.

It has almost become legendary both in the academic and religious camps, that Peter was not only one of the pioneers of Neverland, but he was the first who spoke of shadows as an inevitable piece of the Whole. Through this revelation it was held that he developed the wisdom to lay-out the architecture of Neverland.

But the image we saw that day was a monster—an anomaly that mutated into an image of terror. Is this the one causing the devastation of Neverland? Is this the reason why Peter has to leave his home?

Before any of us can utter a word, Peter spoke:

> I was hooked up last night to a virtual reality program I designed for self-therapy. It was fine, until the virus become uncontainable. There were so many of them. Like plaguing demons, it invaded the shack. I fought with barely any strength left and with a sword dulled by years of false certainty. They entrapped me on a massive web so they could devour my flesh and blood. Then I woke up. It was only a dream, a simulation, an augmented world.

"Pete, dark clouds are gathering everywhere! What the hell happened to Neverland?" asked Neil aggressively.

Peter continued saying,

> Neverland was not meant to be another project, not at all. It was an aftermath of the growing discontent with past stockades and stagnancy, directives and certainty, exclusivism and fakery. There was so much tiredness with speeches that were filled with demonizing rhetoric; or global policies that were engineered by advanced economies; or churches that were more concerned with antiquity than relevance.
>
> So some of us formed a global networking less classified by fences and borders; where technology fosters democratic communication and neutrality; where authenticity is celebrated and not read as occupational liability; where a vocational student in Bolivia can have the same social space privileges with an executive in New York.
>
> I mean, what's up with the Silents and Boomers and their oppressive regimes, dogmatism, tribal warfare, male dominance, carbon emissions, terrorism? Can we not have a human

community that is not threatened by mass migration but celebrates the beauty of diversity? Where sacred texts are not use to stereotype an emerging woman? Where we can flatten business pyramids and decentralize control? Where we don't just narcotize spiritual brokenness, but create poetry, philosophy, or new paths out of them? Where conservation is not another greenwashing scheme but a genuine reconnection with our biosphere? Where the formulation of sciences is not confined within the observatories and academic halls of the West?

I mean the Cold War is history, and we don't need a new enemy to promote patriotism; or more wars to fund militarism; or more grand tales to assume dominance over others!

So gradually, here and there, there were sparks, diversions, innovations, expeditions; and new blueprints, embryos, microchips, biofuels; barricades, emigrations, interfaces, multidimensions.

They were cutting edge, deconstructing, posteinsteinian, cyber-uprising!

And without us being consulted, your people called us Pans and our work, Neverland. The world was fascinated with all the magic enveloping our houses. But for us, it is really not about the magic. It's about having a home. Our houses are now spread globally, defying the law of locality. But like a cyber-society, we are interconnected by radio waves, time, and stories.

Unlike past communities, where houses were built with prearranged shapes and dimensions, restrictions were removed so diversity and discovery can prosper. And it did. There were cubical cods, cylindrical chattels, spherical snouts, pentagonal patios, multi-colored prisms, a peripteral pad, a claustral cottage, and other geometric weirdness.

Entire walls were usually glass—patterned, clear, stained, and frosted. Some glass walls are transparent across and translucent when looking from above. Roofs have an installed renewable energy contraptions from solar panels, wind turbines, to hydropower gutters.

It is not unusual to see holographic images displayed by the patio, or beamed 200 feet above the roof, or covering the entire house, creating an illusion of a post-apocalyptic landscape, or a fictional medieval castle, or Star Trek's tacky space station.

The interior setup ranges from extreme minimalism to extravagant neo-victorianism. Some things are common though: hi-tech computer gadgetry, state of the art appliances, advanced automations, and exploding sound systems.

But if the magical is really sought after here, that's not even a fraction of the hat. The real object of fascination is not the house. It is the transcendental interconnection between them. Like ligaments to the body, or gravity to the universe, there is a narrative, an epoch, an unseen artery that interweaves each home.

As you can see, everything was well, until reports of shadow outbreaks and homes that turned haunted, started coming in. Then some pipelines between houses got major clogging, while residences that were relocated at the fringe slowly deteriorated. Their owners left. It's like a ghost town in some places and its spreading fast.

This is not an extinction scenario. A huge percentage of our online communities are still holding their ground. And as one of the Pans of Neverland, desertion was far from my options.

But then . . . then I saw my own shadow.

Fear took a strong grip and did not let go—the fear of defeat, demolition, and disheartening the hopefuls.

I tried hiding it. But I was not aware that someone was watching me in the dark that night. It was a young zeeker and her eyes were filled with a hundred questions. And so I ran away. Not because of the fear to be exposed, but because of the guilt I felt knowing that I was already demonstrating the same hypocrisy I fought with when I was young. And so I've been hiding here for a few days now with this pathology, this anomaly, this Shadow.

Paul with his comforting pastoral demeanor spoke saying,

> Peter, this is not the end. God can wash away sins as red as crimson. But we need to treat things as it is. This is not just an inaccuracy, an anomaly, or a pathology for artists to unlock their creativity. This is sin, transgression, desecration! But through repentance, you will experience regeneration.
>
> By his retribution and resurrection, you are offered redemption; and through rebirth, you go through divine adoption. This is not about religion. This is about you and God in a glorious

reconciliation. Shadows will vanish and all fear of condemnation.

I'm all for reform and innovation. But there is just too much pluralism that promotes paganism, and syncretism that leads to defiant humanism. Like abortion and temple desecration, or munipalization and bloated constitutions. You can't be too prodigal and not end up homeless. Or too revolutionary and not lose your creed.

You are not given a vast biome to shelter humanity, but small arms to embrace a few elected. We cannot cure the world of sin, we can only trust the ethereal wisdom of predestination.

If you trust these words, then also trust God's presence being here. He wants to make your heart his dwelling, if you are willing for him to come in. This glorious experience is as easy as saying a simple prayer of acceptance. Will you all please join me in prayer now?

Era blustered her disagreement saying,

> Whoa! Just hold it right there! I believe in Christ's redemptive work; am too a recipient of that eternal Grace you just spoke of. I confess my sin of silence before injustice, and my sin of praise while my city was in grief.
>
> But I cannot be part of a prayer that diminishes God to clockwise fatalism. Or a judgment-seat-invocation that delivers a verdict to the alleged damned and elected. I do not worship the god of Crow and Calvin nor go to the temples of Caiaphas and the crusaders.
>
> I know it's just a prayer, but have we not learned from the past how poisonous still reli-

gion is, when induced with toxic truth-claims? Did we not heed the prophetic call of postmodernity? Did we not inscribe their counsel on our class syllabus, songs, and monuments?

Can we not hear anymore with our conscience the cries of countless preys, who were slain under the metal cross of Inquisition, or killed by hateful Jihads, or slaughtered by ethnic cleansing blades—all started by one imprecatory prayer? And then advanced by a twisted theology that promotes one's religious superiority over another?—Scriptures above paganism; conservatism over syncretism; Jerusalem surpassing all holy cities?

I may be guilty of overreacting, but please hear me well.

Peter carries a great extent of influence. He is a glimpse of tomorrow's human community. And today, he is experiencing a new birth. Whatever we say and he absorb today will have a great impact on his personal unfolding, and the terrains, societies, humanity, he and his cohorts will create, and we all will wake up to the morning of our future existence. Do you all understand?

And Paul, can you please cut off with your pious rhymes and intonation. You don't sound more holy by not talking normally.

Paul responded saying,

Oh Era, Era, Era . . . of all people I would expect you to be more appreciative of the art of homily; or to be on edge with history!

Of all people, I would expect you to have a wider embrace! What, is my belly really too big for your ecumenical hug? Or am I barred from your kumbayah fellowship because I'm a Republican? I agree with Neil. It's not hard to get bothered by your hypocrisy. I mean, who really is the devious, the exclusivist, the one intoxicated with truth-claims?

And wait, were you not his closest mentor on architectural experimentation? Were you not the nagging skeptic in his head when he sat quietly on church pews? Did you slash half of your history book so you can easily incriminate religion in your eco-friendly but hate-filled diatribe? Tell me, where are the lost pages of Gandhi, Luther King, Mother Theresa, Nightingale, or C. S. Lewis?

Or how about those thick chapters on the codification of democracy, abolition of slavery, and the establishment of hospitals and universities? Did you not teach him the parameters of self-determination and the heart of respecting the elderly? Did Peter become too airborne that he lost his ability for earthly good?

Look, you obviously made great strides in developing Neverland. You quilted flags and sponsored treaties; led expeditions and reformed immigration; built bridges and virtual highways; taught Peter aerodynamics and showed him places beyond the familiar and its gravitational pull.

But while you plant trees you also uproot customs; while you recycle bottles you also thrash our constitution; while you harness the sun you also betray our faith by worshipping it. But Peter, yes even Peter Pan needs permanence.

> He needs to go home, stay there, and invite Jesus
> in. That's all I'm saying.
> Wait, I think Miriam wants to say something.

"No, actually," Miriam answered. "I was just gesturing to Era about her spices. I don't really have anything to say right now. Did you bring the spices?"

Era reached inside one of her lower pockets and handed to Miriam a bottle of seasoning.

Unaware of how untimely her topic was with the present tension, she explained quite ardently, "This is a five-spice powder that came from five separate lands, blended together to create this distinct taste of sour umaminess balanced with rich sweetness.... Uhm, uhm... which... I'm ... sure... none of you are interested right now... to know. Sorry. Would you excuse me please?"

With a weak voice and almost groping for words, Era conceded to Paul saying, "I think you are right... I'm sorry Paul. Peter, I'm sorry too. You may need to go home for a while. If you think you still need me, I will help you in your renovation. Just try not to make a house as 'unimaginative' as Paul."

Neil seemed so disappointed with what he just heard. Again he threw some tough words. "That's just a bunch of bull crap! Not you Miriam!"

Miriam was quick in reacting, "I know. Because you know you will not be getting anything from my kitchen if you were talking about me!"

Neil smiled and said, "I know."

He then turned to Era and raged,

But you Era, what you just did, was the most pathetic display of weakness I've seen in a while! What happened to the Era I disputed with this morning who was enflamed with unwavering axioms? Oh, I forgot! You are incapacitated by the "world peace" disease. You know, I like you but you don't really have the balls to push for a real global revolution.

You talk of the poison of organized religion. But talk is all you do! And yes, you sing your kumbayah, drive a Prius, and mastered some yoga poses. And then you wait for something to happen.

You have a strategic access to lawmakers and trailblazers. You carry a placard, the techiest smart phone, and two doctoral titles after your name. You wear the hottest eco-clothing and speak the latest political jargon. And again, you wait for something to happen.

What are you afraid of, offend somebody and loose your "peace-maker" reputation? This whole world is headed for extinction, if we don't do something severe to neutralize the poison!

Bloody was the Civil War undeniably, but it cured the early fragmented America and turned it into the United States we have now.

Infinitely vast is the impact of a dying star, but planets are not formed without the dust particles provided by such massive bang! Bang! Bang!

Brutal was the crucifixion of Christ, but your own gospel justifies the compelling need for a sacrificial lamb so our Paul here can wear a pious

> smile while he waves around his non-refundable salvation ticket!

Paul quickly retorted back saying, "Take it easy drifter. Just back off a little bit now."

"No you back off you self-righteous swine!" shouted Neil.

Before Paul actually landed any of his punches, Era stood in the middle of the heat to intervene. Neil stepped back steadily with his hands behind his head, strongly clenched on the grip of his blades in his back scabbard. I gently tapped his shoulder, which seemed to calm him down. As Miriam was dragging him to the kitchen, he hurled his last dispute.

> Pete, what did they do to you? How did you end up in here? You don't deserve this. You used to carry your sword like a man. All of you did! You all bought tools from my armory for your demystification, reformation, deconstruction, occupation, civilizing mission, deculturalization, militarization, abolition! And what did you gave me in return? Denunciation!—using the very weaponries I gave you! You traitors!
>
> "Pete, I know your father. We used to level shadow-cities together. I can see his eyes in you! You are a warrior. You know in your blood that the time of building is not today. There is a war out there and your very existence is at stake. Draw your sword, or here . . . please take mine!
>
> But whatever you do, don't do this! Don't do nothing!"

Though the kitchen was a complete mess when we entered it, it was filled with a captivating aroma that rose from a boiling soup.

"Did you bring some ghosts with you?" Miriam asked Neil.

Neil responded defiantly, which seemed to upset Miriam a lot. Without warning, Miriam twisted Neil's right arm, pushed him against the wall, took his swords, and threatened him with further pain if he will not cooperate.

"I don't have time to explain. I need some ghosts now!"

I was confused, until Neil pulled out a pouch that contains some red powdered spice. Miriam was only referring to Neil's ghost pepper, also known as Bhut Jolokioa, a chili pepper once recognized as the fieriest in the world. In the hands of someone like Neil, these things can be lethal. In Miriam's kitchen, well, it's edibly exquisite. She poured the whole pouch, which I assumed is roughly 7 grams.

"Isn't that a little strong?" I asked.

"Not if you brought some of the leaves I asked you about," Miriam answered.

I reached inside my bag to give her some leaves from my bamboo tree. That was the last ingredient needed for her soup.

After a while, we felt another trembling, but this time a bit stronger. She seemed to be more anxious yet somehow comforted by the luscious aroma ascending from her now completed musht soup. Then we heard a commotion from where the others were gathered.

Neil and I hurriedly went back, and when we got there, Era was holding Peter in her arms. "Peter is dying," she cried.

Like a bad serum, helplessness invaded our nerves. And while distraught with this feeling, I noticed two things. First, the instability of the shack was somewhat related to Peter's declining condition. Second, at that crucial hour, Miriam was once again missing, engrossed as usual with her culinary ambitions.

I looked in his eyes again. This time, I saw myself in my own shack weeks ago when death was at the edge of winning. "It will take a miracle," I said to myself. He was almost gone.

Though gripped by fear, Paul was still hopeful for a miracle. A big guy with a soft shepherd's heart, he went to the place where he was best at: his knees. Looking at him, my mind was filled with bible scenes that describe the miraculous. What if deliverance comes like the parted sea, or when dry deserts meet a bountiful river flow? Or like the days when prophets were fed by ravens, or when barren wombs were opened, or when a bad fishing trip can turn into a resurrection encounter? Seeing Paul in groaning intercession heightened my faith to whisper once more that old prayer song, "Do it again, Lord, do it again!"

Neil, on the other hand only knew one posture during dangers or threats—rogue vigilance! With a vicious grin on his face and sharp blades on both hands, he was ready for war—even if he had to start one. But even with paranoia as bad as Neil's, his sincerity could still overshadow all his delusional antics. He was doing it all for Peter.

And then there was Era. Her compassion was a spiritual portrayal of Michelangelo's *Pieta*, as she held his dying nephew on her arms, wrapping his bitter body on a quilted cloak. She will shield him from any harm, be it her life the price for his salvation.

Peter was tightly holding a cross pendant, which seemed to be broken at the base. He had told me earlier that his father gave it to him when was 12, right before the old man had gone missing.

I used my hammer to reinforce a few damaged poles, so we could buy more time, if we needed to evacuate. But it was not gonna happen. Because just as the walls around us were collapsing, a toxic fume was released from the wound of the fallen shadow, filling the air with a frightening, fatal cloud.

"Well, see you all in hell, comrades," yelled Neil.

Then out of the blinding fog, Miriam came out carrying a big pot. As if unaffected by all the chaos around us, she poured some soup in a bowl, sprinkled it with some magic dusts, and asked Era to help Peter take a sip. Remarkably, we immediately saw some sign of relief. We were all amazed of how instant the healing was from that homemade kitchen soup. But then it was also Miriam's.

The shaking stopped, and the fog slowly dissipated. Then Miriam gave everyone a bowl. It was awesome. It was almost psychedelic to say the least. I don't know what others felt, but my awareness was somewhat heightened.

"So what's up with this soup?" asked Paul.

Miriam explained,

> In the beginning God made a primordial soup. At least that is what classical physics would say. There are of course other recent theories on the origin of life. But what can I say, I'm old school. Plus, I love the kitchen metaphor, especially

when God is the one cooking. Anyway, since then it has always been soup.

Whenever a society, or even the whole human community in that respect, comes to a grave spiritual hunger, God writes a new soup recipe. And luckily there will always be someone who will be stupid enough to read it, gather the ingredients, and cook! After all, what's a house without a hot delicious home-made soup on a stormy winter night?

"So is this one of your chicken soup for the soul series? Neil interrupted. "I bet Paul is behind this!"

Miriam responded saying, "Well yes and no! No, this is not another chicken soup reruns, nor is this Jessica Simpson's 'chicken of the sea' product. I mean if you watch any reality TV, no? Don't worry about it. But yes, Paul brought the main ingredient. He brought the St. Peter fish. Yes, this is a medicinal fish soup."

I believe that everyone felt a sense of holiness pervading the room as we proceeded with the meal. But unlike the sorrow of the Last Supper, the sacredness lay in the celebration of healing, and the gift of humor in somewhat sanctifying the hands of God's undeserving healers.

Unexpectedly however, the smoke started rising again to a point of chilling blindness. But this time, no one moved. When the fog settled, we were already in another place. We asked among ourselves where we were.

"We are still here. The same place; just different in time period. About 50 years ago to be exact," Miriam explained.

Neil sneered slightly and asked, "What the hell did you put in that soup?"

"Well, aside from all of your ingredients, I put a little magic mushroom, you know just enough for us to have this tour."

"You sorcerer!" Paul screamed.

Miriam smiled and replied quite sarcastically, "Aww, thank you, I appreciate that."

"But that's not possible. This was an observatory for many years," Era objected.

> Yes, but if you go further back, this was a water reservoir. Travelers discovered an aquifer underneath us and decided to settle here. They dug wells, and erected water towers for agricultural and distribution purposes. The population grew and nearby villagers came and received their share of nature's generosity.
>
> Accompanying this expanding oasis however was a thirst unquenched by water. The thirst of greed deceived many in accentuating issues of governance and ownership over the joy of community and simplicity. Soon, legal disputes replaced barrio feasts; our bond with earth was severed by facilities and factories; and the groundwater abandoned for artificial reservoirs.
>
> A few years later, a group of college students received some funding to renovate this place and turn it into a multifunction observatory, intended to study the reported gas emissions from a dormant volcano nearby.
>
> But their fascination was lured away from lavas and rock samples, to the beauty of celestial objects that were seen through their colossal optical telescopes. Needless to say, they too were disconnected from the ground.

And then without any warning, we were once again shifted to another space-time.

Paul with an anxious voice, grumbled, "Miriam, would you mind telling us what planet is this, because I've a feeling we're not in Kansas anymore."

Miriam answered saying,

> Well, first I just want to let you know that I forgive you for using that cheesy overplayed line. Second, yes this is not your typical 'Kansas.' We are inside the virtual blueprint of Peter's shack. So that explains the computer-aided topography, mechanical drawings, and the blue ground you are standing on.
>
> Directly in front of us is the side view foundation plan of the facility beneath the water station, where tunnels and huge water pipes connect the groundwater to the surface.
>
> Also, the footing, installations, base walls, anchor bars and bolts as you can see, are made visible. Normally however, these things are hidden or ignored. People just get their water without knowing the processes beneath the ground. Because they feel that they don't need to, and someone else always gets it for them.
>
> But this place was only meant to be a model, so people will learn to get reconnected with their own land, and dig their own well. Unfortunately, the model expired before learning took place: learning, for laying down foundations that are meant to hold additional floors; learning, for reconnecting with dirt and water as the source of both grains and beingness; learning, for the recovery of buried wisdom of past and aged

homeowners, so as to see and experience the cross in its totality.

Yes, for now, the cross is what we know.

And Peter, there is a deeper reason why your father gave you that cross. It is not just an ancient religious symbol. The cross is a representation of the Whole we are all desperately searching for. The upper section represents psycho-spirituality, consciousness, our inherent need for God, pietism, religion.

The line, from one side to another, symbolizes the horizontal reality that connects all creation—relationships, societies, shared values, ecosystems, cultures, compassion, languages, integrity, homes.

The lower portion of the cross is the shadow section or our sinful humanity, or the anti-matter, the unknown, our painful past, outdated lies, old nature, disease, deformity, demise.

For Paul, it's sin, Satan, and 'lazy liberals.'

For Era, it's probably carbon emissions.

For Neil, I guess it's the shrinks and the pacifists, or Oprah and Dr. Phil.

In Ferdie's life, it's that old creepy basement.

For you, well for you Peter it is . . . it is mostly your parents. . . .

Like the wars your fathers created with their delusion of exceptionalism, labeling some of your fb friends as a social menace. Or their institutional postures that only emits hypocrisy, disconnect, and their unwillingness to change. Or their way of departmentalizing the populace by age in schools, workplaces, and churches.

Or it can be you—your hatred towards them.

> Peter, do you know why Neverland is having these problems? Because most of you did not dig enough! You expanded crosswise and skyward, but you neglected the ground. You avoided excavation because you thought that the soil is dirty, contaminated by your parents and your past.
>
> You believed that you can afford such disconnection because you are the Peter Pan generation—the airborne, self-reliant, cyber-wizards! And so your foundation was compromised. But a cross will not stand without the base firmly grounded, will it Peter? Peter?

After hearing no reply, we realized that Peter was not with us anymore. The blue ground we were walking on was ruthlessly engulfing him. We grabbed his hands and with all our strength and tried to pull him out. But the force beneath was too strong.

"What in the world was that?" cried Era. "Will he get hurt? Miriam, we need to go get Peter home now!"

Miriam answered Era but with her eyes fastened at me, "But we are, we are home always already."

Suddenly, the virtual environment dissipated, giving us back the murky metal walls of the shack we were in. In the center was Peter gasping for breath, exhausted but a slight smile was peering out.

He then told us what happened.

> I was underground, held gently by an old beaten hand. There I saw rock formations designed by meteor impacts and magma ruins; fastened by countless sunlights, prepared to carry sanctuaries and citadels, mansions and skyscrapers, bridges and highways, nations and kingdoms.

I was inside that fortress of strength, accuracy, stability, and I felt both suffocation and fascination towards it.

After a while there was water up to my knees, and it was rising fast. All of a sudden, the rock beneath me broke open, and the hand holding me let go. It was more than a 70 feet fall with what seemed to be an underground river below. It was flowing.

But before I touched the water, I saw people standing by the shoreline. They were trying to stop the flow. Some built dams, others threw rocks, and there were those who discharged pollutants.

Some created overbearing doctrines, others designed cold hierarchies, and wrote cruel ethnocentrism. But empires continued falling; sciences kept on altering claims; constitutions from all lands were amended; gravity still won; death stank; their names forgotten.

In their futile attempt, some were taken by the current. Those standing by the shore tried to help, but they too got caught. So the rest stayed away from it and hated the flow even more. Some drowned. I saw them die in the cruel force of the raging waters.

As I fell nearer to the surface of the river, I saw a startling sight. There were those who emerged from the depths. Like newly baptized believers after immersion, their faces glowed. For they did not contend with the turbulence anymore; they simply drifted, float, flow. . . .

And then instantly, I was swallowed in its oblivion. I kicked and stroked while I submerged deeper. The fear of uncertainty was more painful than drowning. After much struggle, I yielded. I was experiencing the pain of death, but the awareness of the experience tells me I'm not dying.

I could breathe. I was conscious. And beneath that river, I started to flow. I knew I needed to ascend to the surface eventually. But I really didn't know how. All I knew was that I was a silent witness to the magic underneath the flow.

After a while the water kept getting warm until the temperature became unbearable. Due to intense heat, almost half the river vaporized and blazing flames invaded the riverbed, transforming it into a burning valley. Engulfed in pain and rage, I screamed for help. But there was none.

Instead the place was filled with loud pounding sounds that echoed above where shadows hide in dark corners of foundations and basements. Like bats disturbed from secret caves, they fled with shrieks and eeks to homeowners, homebuilders, and the dispersed homeless above.

I followed the source of the sound until I saw an old man, hammering something metal on a huge anvil. He was pounding on what seemed to be my own sword, smithing it to be turned to something else. But the stronger his beating was, the higher the flame rose.

I begged for him to stop, but he wouldn't listen. I was angry, but anger just fueled more fire. I gave up and asked him, "Why are you doing this?"

He stopped and came towards me to give my sword back. But it was not a sword anymore. It was a foundation anchor bolt, firm and well-crafted. Without him speaking a word, I think I understood what he meant and I believe I saw who he really was. My eyes were opened.

And so I asked, "Why am I so disconnected from you, from them? Why can't we be one home again?"

He then told me, "But there is only one cross, always already. And I failed in the past to show this to you Peter. I'm so sorry. Really, I am. I'm just glad you made it down here."

He reached out his hand to touch the cross I was wearing. The damage vanished and the bottom piece was restored.

And then he said, "Are you ready Simon?"

"For what," I asked.

"To fly home!"

And then a whirlwind came and carried me back here.

I don't know much of what just happened and I'll be lying to you if I say that I am now completely free of hatred. But this inner peace with my deficiency to conceive and forgive tells me that I'm sincerely trying, and it reminds me of who I am—that I am both Simon Peter and Peter Pan, a child of heaven and a resident of the middle ground.

I guess I've been riding in the wind for so long that I have forgotten the stability of rocks, the wisdom of water, and the gift of fire that my parents sparked. But now I know that I am home at the foot of the cross.

As he was talking, everyone noticed that the wound of the shadow was slowly closing. And from a beastly figure it went back to its original shade-form.

And so I asked myself, "Did these Shadows turn berserk because they were just troubled by the situation below?" Like daunting ghosts with unfinished issues, they ascended from the depths of the earth to warn us of the danger beneath, but we all misjudged the message of these unusual messengers.

Everyone was silent, almost all were looking at Miriam waiting for her response. But there was none. Something else took her attention. The small sunray that peeked inside the shack invited her to come out. We all followed her outside and were completely startled with what we saw.

We were in Neverland.

With a tone of both wonder and frustration Paul asked, "So you mean to tell me that everything that happened there, including the fish soup and all, was virtual? None of them were real?"

Neil responded, "The bigger question is, how do we even know we're already in the real world right now?"

Era was the least concerned.

"But what's the difference, really? I mean real or not, that soup was amazing," she answered.

Everyone seemed to agree.

While they were still talking, I decided to follow Miriam all the way to the lake.

Mesmerized by the beauty of trees dressed in autumn leaves, beauty that covers the land with provision and enchantment, she stood at the edge of a precipice where the forest is revealed in its entirety. She continued walking until she reached the lake. Weary, she sat motionless, aware of the troubled water in front of her, yet unaffected. I saw her immersed as an observer of life, silently watching it flow through unseen currents like time, gravity, change.

Around her, the misty grass responded with glee to the sun that awakened it with beams of morning greeting announcing a new day was here. She touched their gentle blades and she seemed to be empowered once again.

No celestial visions. No decorous rituals. No eloquence or brilliance. Only a child-like fascination of what *Is*. In that awareness, she is home in the embrace of the eternal *I Am*, whom she beautifully embodies.

It was already Sunday morning.

I slowly approached her, purposely stepping on some dry leaves, just enough for her to hear me coming. "I did not know you were married," I said teasingly. "Maybe I should meet him sometime."

"Maybe you already did," she replied. "He's a blacksmith."

"Why do you do this?" I asked. "I mean always talking in parables?"

"Don't we all do it?" she asked with a face so surprised or she was just being cynical.

> Oops, sorry, I did it again right? What can I say? I guess when you get this old, the line gets a bit blurry—you know, between maps and territory, or between facts and fables, or between blueprints and houses. Soon you'll start to realize that the thoughts, words, and experiences you ascribe as actuality are just but partial representations of the Whole that you and I still do not

> know. So one day you just give up the quest for accuracy and end up like me— transcendentally strange!
>
> Add some confusing parables into it and people will actually think that you are enlightened.

We both had a good laugh after that odd "word of wisdom."

"But seriously Ferdie, truth is beautiful when implied," she added.

She then turned her eyes to the lake and said, "Listen, I have some friends coming over to pick me up. Do you need a ride?"

"No thanks, I have a train to catch, if you know what I mean," I replied. She looked at me wittily, but before she was able to say, "fast learner," her boat appeared on the horizon. It was the same boat she and her students were building just a few days ago when I saw them in a field near the train carriage I squatted in when I was homeless.

As the boat was leaving, she was still yelling some words. Though I could barely hear her, I think I got one right. "Go home and start making soup!"

I sat down, weary as the others are, overwhelmed with the things I had seen and heard the past three days. But I think I know what I need to do and what to give Peter. And if you are reading this, it would mean he accepted my gift to him.

I don't know who you are and what you're going through, but if my story connects with yours, then this is probably providence. I hope I've been faithful in this humble task of reflecting on the journey of restless seekers I see around and inside me. I pray that through this poetic narration, a glimpse of that shrouded path, a crisis I call homelessness, glimmered through the words, and across the pages of this journal.

In whatever case, it's been an honor journaling with you. Please receive this farewell benediction from a weary spiritual shepherd:

> Blessings to the Restless
>
> To the restless who dared life's second half, and went outside the familial or institutional box. To fellow travelers who stumbled by the wayside—weary of the rat race, but so afraid to stop and cry, 'timeout!' To those who are fed up with flat worlds that are maintained by broken systems; or to visionaries whose hopes are bigger than the status quo.
>
> To those whose curiosity transcends doctrines, decrees and dead legalism, or those who can't adapt to a life of permanence or spiritual plateau. Like a physicist who sees beyond a Newtonian model, or a pastor sick and tired of playing church.
>
> To a high school teacher whose commitment is deeper than a paycheck, or a legislator whose integrity transcends party aisles. To the idealist, the perfectionist, the dreamers who can't conspire with apathy, or those who would not know what a suburban backyard is.
>
> To students who are undaunted to ask questions, or moms bigger than office cubicles and kitchen tables. To the inventor, the innovator, the impulsive, the poet, the painter, the prophet, the hitchhiker, the hungry, the hunter; to the cynic,

the curious, and all those infected with dire discontent.

To the restless who wander in the wilderness without a mentor and a map, who run with little direction, who walk in darkness without a lamp, who are justifiably angry, or who because of pain can only converse in paintings and poetries.

Like a cancer survivor who is facing a relapse, or a family on the brink of a painful breakdown. Or like a gray-haired veteran who went to a geriatric facility this morning, or a single mom who waits on a welfare line.

To the restless. . . .

May your uniqueness be vindicated by your character, may your originality shine as inspiring as daylight. May your audacity be appreciated and not barred, and may your deviations not be taken as sourgraping or deliberate drags.

And because of your passion, may you create new sparks of enthusiasm, because of your seeking, may you create new paths. Because of your courage may you awaken hope, in the midst of a people devastated by past letdowns.

But also fellow restless, along the way may you develop contentment even with imperfection, and an acceptance of mysteries that will not yield; to climb mountains when they won't move, and to pause for a day or two before climbing any of them.

Because there are cross roads along the way—they are life-altering, while ironically heart-rending. To move on, choices will be made, paradigms will be altered, souls will be gravely expanded: a painful process of letting go; a period of rebirth; a place of death.

So we can understand that true happiness will require that we live today and forgo some benefits of projection. There your soul will demand balance, and the thrill of elevation will seek your willingness to be hidden for a while.

May there be peace in your soul before calmness in your storm. May lessons be learned before solutions. May failure be a fertile soil where seeds of wisdom are planted; trusting God's hands, and yielded to events you cannot alter.

Don't try expelling these seasons of uncertainty. They are necessary. Because we who are restless can only learn to live a full life when we slow down—after an injury, during a crisis, or when we are too depressed to run. Then and only then we experience the joy and meaning of stillness. For there we meet with the One who promised,

"Come home, those of you who are tired and I will give you rest."

I need to stop. Someone is behind me and I think I know who he is. Farewell, for now.

Conclusion

I Am Not Ferdie Anymore

"How are you Simon?" I asked as I turned to look at him.

"I'll be fine," he replied.

"Except this, I cannot really give you anything," I said, as I handed him my journal. "It's not finished yet. You can do with it what you think is best. You can continue writing it or you can discard it after reading."

He gave me back my pen and said, "I won't be needing this." He smiled reminding me that he's a millennial.

"Where are you headed?" Peter asked.

Before I was able to answer him, the cross that he was wearing caught my attention once more. Its physical form was not different from a tree. Its torso unconditionally bridged ground and heaven. And like branches, its arms extended infinitely across creation, bearing eternal life and baring the Savior's love.

"I'm going home," I replied.

With his eyes beaming with wholeness, he said "But you already are!"

If this is one of those cheesy summer movies, the camera will dramatically zoom out, capturing the whole terrain

I Am Not Ferdie Anymore

where the shack is located, showing the cross-like layout of the abandoned observatory, and an open lake on its right side.; but going further, Neverland is revealed with its fascinating architectures and interconnection, somewhat altered due perhaps to its better tie with the ground; and ascending higher to heaven, this imaginary camera is now presenting the massive sphere we call home, with shacks, shelters, and societies connected together by open vines.

But the camera keeps on moving away, now shooting from the nearest moon outside the range of our host star, where the planets are portrayed like spiral pods calmly hanging from vast lustrous branches.

Like an all-seeing eye, the camera now covers the entirety of the universe. But instead of showing a spherical or hyperbolic vastness, it shows a tree--the tree of life that bears clusters of stars and galaxies in their different stages of evolution.

Against my will, the camera goes beyond the boundary of knowledge. Having no words, images, nor thoughts, it shows the bamboo plant.

It cycles back.

The music gradually fades. There is silence, while the screen slowly shows the words, "the end."

But this is not a film. This is a journal.

Which reminds me, that I need to clarify that this is not Ferdie, not anymore. The last 388 words are already mine. This is Peter.

I still use Ferdie's voice and writing style, hoping that this is how he wants the chapter to end. But this is not the end of the journal. Starting today, I will start writing the next chapter.

I challenge you to write, express, and narrate, with me—stories of meaninglessness, questions that led to absurdity, wounds that turned fatal, or homelessness that still seeks for an open door. Ferdie gave us a sample, now it's time for you and me to create our own.

I know it's not going to be easy. I myself have a holo-conferencing coming up with some zeekers and boomers, pans and x'ers, and I still don't know what to tell them.

But the memoiring must continue, and we have to do it our way—in blogs, in songs, graffiti, in poems, oil painting, photography, short films, street krumps, culinary, liturgy, in placards, fashion, or martial arts.

From where I am seated, I can feel the force of transformation invading hearts and city gates, minds and markets, borders and belief systems.

But I can also hear the loud screeching of conflicts in public squares and warblogs, generating new forms of blathering eviler than bombs. Constancy resists, change persists, thus, casualties increased. Casualties like you and me who Ferdie once called "displaced."

But between our shacks, dumps, and cardboards, we can tell our stories in arts and metaphors that ushers healing to the larger world that is now starting to go through a painful transformation.

And through this collective sharing of our narratives, somehow we may learn to experience together the entirety of the cross and be able to build houses in whole.

And with that, I think I know the first thing I'll say later tonight:

"Welcome, fellow residents of one household.

The table is ready.

Our main course for tonight, I made soup.

Welcome home!"

Epilogue

Reflective Writing Process

There are several brilliantly written books out there that give a step-by-step guideline on successful memoir writing. This book is not of them, or, more so this section.

Rather, this epilogue is a short description of the writing processes I used—processes that mostly came to me randomly as I immersed in the practice of journaling.

Hopefully, readers will find some of the items below insightful, and discover their inherent values in their own writing experiences.

1. ***Let it flow.*** I write my journal without too much analytical assessment of the subject. Instead, I allow my emotions and thoughts to emerge almost randomly, so I can freely put them into words. I temporarily suspend any form of mental judgment or proofreading, whether it's theological, grammatical, or ethical. And then when needed, I edit my entries afterwards.

2. ***Don't let a moment pass.*** I don't usually schedule my journaling. The need or motivation to write comes at any given time under any circumstances. Whether I journal using an ipad application, or I'm writing on an

empty cereal box, I don't allow a spark of inspiration to pass without chronicling it.

3. ***Just write***. Also, I don't wait for a dramatic event or an intense emotion to come before writing. When my existential crisis was severe, reflecting on the actuality of common things, devoid of fancy adjectives, was immensely therapeutic. At one time, while my son was snoring at the back seat of the car, totally sacked out, I wrote about a light pole, a pile of snow, and a seagull in front of my parking spot. I sat in silence as I write words and breathe the simplicity of that present moment.

4. ***Get honest***. I don't write as an author, not during the initial journaling phase. I write with no readers or potential publishers in mind. When writing is personal, I attain a level of honesty where journaling becomes therapeutic. I only have readers or hearers in mind when I'm already preparing a journal entry to be used in a homily, poetry, essay, or book.

5. ***Go back***. I go back to past entries to reflect them with present ones, or sometimes to edit them, or continue writing about a former topic. Sometimes what I wrote in the past is still relevant to the things that I'm going through right now, and so I go back to old pages occasionally for self-encouragement.

6. ***Keep it intimate***. Most entries are not meant to be shared with outside readers. Details are so sensitive and confidential at times, that the writer should filter wisely the entries to publicize and the items to keep. In most cases, most will remain intimate.

7. **Share it**. However, there may be some details that the writer could consider sharing with a therapist or spiritual mentor. Because reflective writing is a form of therapy, insights from a trained counselor will provide additional benefits. I myself had the privilege of receiving spiritual direction from my mentor, on journal entries I cannot personally analyze or explore.

8. **Drop the cookie cutter**. I did not follow one method and I did use one voice in journaling. I can write as first, second or third person, entering texts as prayers, poetries, stories, essays, or quotes. In this field of writing, the freedom to innovate is more extensive than systems in other writing genre.

9. **It takes time**. Journaling as a therapy is a process that may take some time to demonstrate certain healing results that the writer may have expected. Though instant relief or insight may occur at times, it takes numerous entries, combined with other forms of therapy, for questions or emotional issues to get resolve.

10. **You are already an expert**. If you can tell a story, then you can write a memoir, and you are the only one adept in journaling your own experiences, ideas, and artistry, shaping it with your own style and personality. And because you are already an expert with your life story, you might as well write about it.

Bibliography

Grof, Stanislav, and Christina Grof. *Spiritual Emergency: When Personal Transformation Becomes a Crisis.* New York: Tarcher, 1989.

www.ingramcontent.com/pod-product-compliance
Lightning Source LLC
Chambersburg PA
CBHW070920180426
43192CB00038B/2053